What People Are Saying...

"Awakened women with the consciousness and capacity to positively shape our world have never been more needed. *Woman, Goddess & Savior* calls on us to liberate our spiritual essence so that we can set ourselves and the world free from the trance of the separate ego. **How rare to have a 'man with heart' such as Richard Axial dedicate himself to awakening the sleeping goddess in women today.** His book is a powerful invitation to accept ourselves just as we are and allow our unique Divine Feminine energy to stream into the world. It is time for women to show up in their fullness, and Richard's book lays out a pathway to do just that."

— Suzanne Anderson, founder of Mysterial Woman and co-author of *The Way of the Mysterial Woman: Upgrading How You Live, Love and Lead*

"*Woman, Goddess & Savior* conveys a deep and important message for our time: **awakening the feminine** and restoring our reverence for the sacred female, a message critical to the health of our species and to the nourishment of our bodies, hearts and souls. Richard offers himself as a wayshower and witness to women seeking awakening. His teachings are at once practical and sober, as well as infused with intimate devotion and surrendered service to the Goddess. **This book is not about transcending to the mountaintop, but about awakening in and through daily life, reveling in the splendor of the feminine creation** and using it as the crucible for enlightenment."

— Stacey Lawson, entrepreneur, author, spiritual teacher
Executive Vice Chairman, Ygrene Energy Fund
Former Board Chair, the Institute of Noetic Sciences

What People Are Saying...

"If you're skeptical about a man offering spiritual lessons to women, you may naturally think twice about reading this book. I say read it anyway! You'll love it as much as me. **This is a sincere and clearly written book that describes a path to spiritual cultivation for Western women.** The author works from the wise insight that the conventional spiritual curriculum has been intended primarily for men. Something different is required for women, in part because we more easily awaken in our daily lives and also because Life needs women at this point in history to awaken! **Richard is an unusually committed champion of Awakened Women** and offers this timely gift in book form. I read the book over the course of a few days, genuinely hungry for what it shared, namely: a narration of Everywoman's journey to know herself as Awake. For this alone, the book is very helpful to the spiritually curious woman. What makes this a truly valuable book, however, is that it is also a call to awakened action by women in general."

—Hilary Bradbury, Ph.D., Member of the Teaching Circle at the Zen Center of Portland, author of *Eros/Power: Love in the Spirit of Inquiry—Transforming how Women and Men Relate*

"Richard Axial has written a profound book. In clear and practical language he illuminates the journey of women awakening to their divine feminine. In my therapy practice I see women who are longing to be more free, embodied and alive. **This book will enhance the lives of all women who read it**, offering tools to free us from self-limiting beliefs and setting us on the path of awakening. Here is to more awake, alive and embodied women!"

—Alice Treves, LCSW
Co-Founder, Stepping Stone Project

What People Are Saying...

"I've always been curious about who I am, what I'm doing here on planet Earth, and I have studied many spiritual practices in order to find a way to live a fulfilling, loving and joyful life. It has sometimes been a lonely journey, and the answers haven't come easily. As a pediatrician of 35 years I have had the honor of listening to parents, especially mothers, who ask these same questions and who are desperately seeking answers in order to find meaning in their lives. ***Woman, Goddess & Savior* revealed a path to me that resonated with my spirit as a woman.** This path of embodied love for others and myself has helped return me to my heart, my joy and a sense of connectedness and purpose. **I recommend this book to any seeker wishing to explore the path of love as a means to enlightenment."**

— **Lindy Woodard, MD, Pediatric Alternatives, Mill Valley, CA, integrative healthcare for children and adolescents**

"Human awakening is at hand... a journey through the spiritual eye of the needle. What's the impetus for such a journey? A powerful energetic in which both women and men evolve beyond ideas of separation, nurture their unique strengths, and **step together into an undivided human consciousness, participating in the evolution of Consciousness itself.** Richard's life work invites women into their powerful place in this awakening, not as by-standers, but rather as the long awaited propulsive force of transformation. Read this book... if you are ready."

— **Deborah Jones, Executive Director, Nine Gates Mystery School**

WOMAN GODDESS & SAVIOR

AWAKENING YOUR DIVINE FEMININE

RICHARD AXIAL

FREE GOD MEDIA

Copyright © 2017 by The Bishop's Trust.

All rights reserved. No part of this publication may be reproduced, distributed or transmitted in any form or by any means, including photocopying, recording, or other electronic or mechanical methods, without the prior written permission of the publisher, except in the case of brief quotations embodied in critical reviews and certain other noncommercial uses permitted by copyright law. For permission requests, write to the publisher, addressed "Attention: Permissions Coordinator," at the address below.

Free God Media
448 Ignacio Blvd, Suite #275
Novato, CA 94949

DISCLAIMER: This publication is a discourse on the topic of spiritual awakening and a commentary on the state of world affairs, and is intended for informational and educational purposes only. With the material contained herein, neither the author nor the publisher claims to offer or provide professional mental health or medical advice, diagnosis or treatment. Individuals in need of these or any other professional services should seek out qualified, licensed practitioners. The practices and processes described in these pages should not be attempted unless the reader is confident of their ability to carry them out, and should seek an expert opinion beforehand if there is any doubt. This material is presented without any guarantee, express or implied, of efficacy or suitability, and no liability is assumed by the author or publisher.

URGENT MESSAGE FROM MOTHER; GATHER THE WOMEN, SAVE THE WORLD © 2005 by Jean Shinoda Bolen used with permission from Red Wheel Weiser, LLC Newburyport, MA www.redwheelweiser.com.

WomanGoddessSavior.com

Library of Congress Control Number: 2017914112

Axial, Richard
Woman, Goddess & Savior: Awakening Your Divine Feminine / 1st ed.
ISBN 978-0-9981774-0-3 paperback edition
ISBN 978-0-9981774-1-0 eBook edition
1. SELF-HELP: Spiritual
2. BODY, MIND & SPIRIT: Inspiration & Personal Growth
3. RELIGION: Spirituality

TABLE OF CONTENTS

INTRODUCTION: Welcome, Dear One 1

PART I: BEING A WOMAN 7
1. Embrace Your Feminine 9
2. Personality and Essence 21
3. Peter Pan World 39

PART II: BECOMING A GODDESS 47
Introduction to Part II 49
4. The Spiritual Path 51
5. A Man's Path or a Woman's Path? 67
6. Working with a Spiritual Teacher 81
7. Spiritual Sisters 91
8. Life, Attention, and the Witness 97
9. Mastering the Ego 105
10. GPS: Your New Compass for Living 119
11. Beauty Is Divinely Deep 133

12. Sex and the Spiritual Girl 141
13. Diving into the Darkness 151
14. The Story of You 157
15. The Ladder of Self-Identity 175
16. Creation and You 185
17. Love that Knows No Limit 201
18. Merging with Spirit 209
19. Communion in Union: The Divine Paradox 219
20. Death and the Divine 223
21. Transcending Ego: Awakening as Oneness 229
22. The Extraordinary Ordinariness of Enlightenment 237

PART III: BECOMING A SAVIOR 243
Introduction to Part III 245
23. Calling All Women 247
24. The Religion of Men 257
25. Birthing the New World 275

Acknowledgments 288
About the Author 290

INTRODUCTION

Welcome, Dear One

Let us set our stage with this statement from the Dalai Lama: *The world will be saved by the Western woman.* His comment stirred up a great deal of discussion and some controversy, yet it highlights an essential issue of our times. The statement also mirrors the sentiment of this book, and it points to why it is important that women take the journey of enlightenment.

Throughout the ages there have been individuals who sought enlightenment, spiritual illumination. We tend to think of this as solely an individual matter; although, when individuals reach this holy state, they often become illuminators and benefactors for an entire society. Think of Buddha, Jesus, Lao-Tsu, Shankara, and countless other luminous or nameless sages who preceded or followed them, and the lasting impact these individuals had on the world around them. Today, many people are seeking enlightenment. While they may benefit personally from their quests, humanity at large is in even more need of such awakened wisdom. We need the guidance of awakened beings, especially awakened women, to chart our course into the future.

"Namaste," the Hindu greeting and farewell, translates into something like, "The god in me recognizes the god in you." It comes from the philosophy that we all have within us a spark of divinity. It honors that we are not mere personalities facing each other, but that each of us has a deeper soul nature that beholds and embraces the other.

I'd like to start by thanking you for having the curiosity and interest to begin this book. I welcome you not from personality to personality or as stranger to stranger, but as two Divine Souls who have always known and loved each other through time and space. I recognize you, whatever your worldly accomplishments and attributes or lack thereof, as the Divine Being, the Goddess. My soul has been longing for you forever. I have yearned to communicate with the person you have become in this birth, to beckon her to her true home and identity as the Goddess. Welcome, Dear One.

This is a book about spiritual awakening, specifically about women's spiritual awakening, an enlightenment that can be realized in the midst of ordinary life. I am a teacher of spiritual awakening, and this book is your invitation to take the journey of enlightenment. It has been my great privilege to welcome women to my spiritual path, to receive them as the Goddess who abides within, and to nourish that Divine spark to its fullness of expression. I offer this as one who has come to know his own inner Divinity and lives as an expression of that Oneness. More than 20 years ago, I left a career in top-level business management to enter the spiritual life, and since then that calling has never left me. After many years of intense spiritual development, I began to teach others, and in the spirit of that teaching I offer this very personal book to you. In the chapter "Embrace Your Feminine" I'll say more about how I came to this calling.

People conduct their lives by presenting to the world around them a personality that they have constructed for "public display," and their primary objective with others is to have this character be accepted and respected. In focusing on this effort, however, it is easy to forget that we are the authors, the creators of this character. And the imaginative, creative person who is thenceforth unacknowledged in the story can often feel unseen and lonely, regardless of the world's response to the invented character.

Not only that, but in living this charade, the deeper levels of your being, whether you are aware of them or not, can also be hidden from you. You are more than the personality you have created. The many levels of your being include:

1. Acted character (the personality you present)
2. Ego (the creator, presenter, and arbiter of that presentation)
3. Authentic individual (you as this alive, natural being behind the mask of ego)
4. True self (your fundamental soul nature)
5. Godhead (you as Goddess)

Conventional life is lived almost entirely at the first two levels, with only occasional glimpses into the authentic self. Psychology also deals with the first and second levels, and sometimes the third. The two deepest levels (true self and Godhead) are almost completely hidden from us, and our culture and society discourage exploration into these depths. Interest in the topic of spirituality can take place at the first two levels, and many people's lives are improved by such inquiries. But it is in the serious pursuit of spiritual awakening—enlightenment—that the dive into our deepest source levels can occur. These are the realms of the Divine.

My gift is to see beyond the character you present, to recognize and honor these deeper levels, and welcome you as all of them. The intention of my work is to open you to your depths—which are already present, though hidden—and encourage their expression. This is the job of the spiritual teacher.

I teach, I guide, I lead, but mostly I listen with an open heart. Whatever skills I possess are not the key, however. The vital core that enables everything is that you are seen by me and are beloved to me. And it is in this state of brotherly love that I offer this book.

Woman, Goddess & Savior is a guide to your deeper regions. Though your journey will be unique, there is a general territory that can be described and offered as guidance for your personal quest. Think of this book, then, as first a tour guide to the land of spiritual fulfillment and second, as an invitation to discover your specific role in joining with other awakened women to steward humanity through its next stage of evolution. You can become one of the midwives who are helping to birth a new species of human.

In many technologically advanced societies, traditional religious affiliation is stagnant or declining while participation in spiritual education is flourishing. Many millions of people in these countries participate in some form of spiritual upliftment. Some may not even know that what they are doing can be considered spiritual, such as yoga or meditation, but others are quite conscious of their spiritual curiosity, interest, or hunger. There is a thriving market for spiritual books and digital media spanning a wide range of perspectives and topics. Many people participate in spiritual workshops and retreats or attend lectures. And the majority of people who participate in these kinds of spiritual activities are women.

Just as there are many people who attend religious services but few who live in monasteries or ashrams, so too are there few people dedicated to the serious work of spiritual awakening. Many people say they are "spiritual," but what they usually mean is that they want a little spiritual peace, love, and comfort in their lives. Few are committed to spiritual development to the point that they are willing to alter their lives significantly in order to pursue more profound spiritual work.

In my teaching, I do not ask people to give up their lives, but, like any spiritual teacher, I prefer to work with people who are committed to their full spiritual evolution. For the women I guide, their desire for spiritual awakening is a passion, not a hobby or mere interest. They have an undeniable hunger or calling for enlightenment. Ordinary life is not fully satisfying; they know there is more to living, and they want it. It is their passion that I serve.

However, the students I teach lead typical lives. They are women of all ages, family situations, and career paths. What they have in common is a very full life. Almost none would be able to leave their life situation behind and enter into full-time spiritual work at some remote seminary, ashram or monastery. So the spiritual practices I teach are designed to be used in the midst of ordinary, modern lives, as you will learn in this book. Today, one need not abandon normal family living in order to become enlightened.

What does it mean to be enlightened? Enlightenment entails a radical change in identity and relatedness. It means you have reached your full evolution as a human; it means god-realization; it means transcending your limited ego identity to experience oneness with existence.

Philosophers, mystics, and spiritual masters throughout the ages have said that this journey of awakening is the greatest adventure an individual can undertake and the greatest service a person can offer to her fellow humans. The journey is our birthright for being born human. I hope that reading this book will inspire you to take this journey, leading with your heart and your hope for humanity, propelled by the hunger for your own self-realization.

In Part I, we will briefly consider whether someone should embark on this journey at all. In Part II we take a fuller look at what spiritual awakening actually means, and I describe how the path that I teach goes about the process of awakening for women. Part III discusses why it is vitally important for humanity that more women awaken to their true spiritual depth and bring their holy love and wisdom to the myriad problems facing humanity.

You've probably read quotes by Gandhi and others similar to this one from Sri Chinmoy: *Do you want to change the world? Then change yourself first.*

I would paraphrase it thusly: "First, change your Self to be the world." So, with that as our guide, we will begin with you.

PART I

BEING A WOMAN

1

Embrace Your Feminine

Let's begin by reviewing some knowledge that I assume we have in common and with which I anticipate you will agree. The terms "women and men" and "feminine and masculine" are not the same. Women and men are used to describe female and male human creatures; whereas, feminine and masculine refer to characteristics those individuals may exhibit. Some characteristics seem to be biologically based, while others are learned from culture. We all have within us both masculine and feminine aspects. Most women have a preponderance of feminine characteristics; that is, they have a feminine polarity. The extent of that feminine dominance can vary greatly from individual to individual, but no woman is 100 percent governed by her feminine characteristics. Likewise for men; most men have a dominant masculine polarity, but the extent of it can vary widely. None of us could function in the world if we could express only our feminine or masculine side.

In referring to feminine and masculine characteristics, I would like to steer clear of the endless debates and stereotypes over exactly what is feminine or masculine. Most ordinary people and academicians alike would agree that such a distinction could be useful, though there may be differences of opinion about specifics. Individuals, of course, have their own unique admixture of these traits.

Likewise, I believe that most people accept that feminine-polarity women and masculine-polarity men are in many ways very different creatures from each other. Thankfully, I feel we have outgrown the once politically correct fad that postulated that men and women are the same and whatever differences there are between them are on the surface and are solely products of culture. In other words, the belief was that we are gender-neutral creatures. A variety of academic disciplines and common knowledge have shown that belief to be false.

"Vive la différence!" I say.

Can a Man Coach a Woman?

Can a man coach a woman? Well, of course he can. Just as a woman can be an excellent coach for a man. But for anyone who may question this, I want to address the matter of why a man is writing a book about the spiritual awakening of women, as I'm sure this could raise legitimate questions from many women. After all, we are just emerging from thousands of years of patriarchal domination of women, and across the world women are still fighting for their basic rights, often in the face of ruthless oppression from men.

In no way do I intend any disrespect to the struggle for women's rights. Indeed, I see myself and my life's endeavors as a champion of those rights, as I hope to demonstrate to the reader in this work.

Let me share a bit about my life. When I was a child living in the U.S. heartland, my mother was the first woman in our small industrial city to enter executive ranks, and I remember well the challenges she spoke about in gaining acceptance and respect in a world of men. Of course in those days, equal pay for women would have been out of the question. During my own executive and consulting career, I directed and worked with many men and women. This work gave me access to a number of brilliant women as employees, colleagues, superiors, and clients. During my work in global development, the organization I worked for was headed by a dedicated woman who was truly a "force of nature." That nonprofit was one of the earliest to recognize that there could be no greater payoff for local and national economic development than to advocate for the empowerment of women. Throughout the developing world, making investments in women, whether through small business microloans, girls' education, or women's civil rights, produces the most consistent results with the lowest resource use. We championed this grassroots strategy instead of the huge development projects that international agencies favored at the time. To this day, empowering women can be the single most effective spur to economic and community development.

In my personal life, I have been fortunate to have loved and been loved. The embrace of women who were fearless and absolute with their love and trust showed me the vast depth of the heart of a woman and its transformative and redemptive power. During the 20-plus years that my life focus has been on the spiritual journey, I learned from both male and female teachers. At some point in my journey of spiritual awakening, the Goddess, the Divine Feminine, embraced me and I have been her devotee and consort ever since. This book is an expression of my homage to Her.

Throughout my life, then, I had opportunities to see how men and women differed in their leadership styles and also to note what it cost them personally, what different stresses they had to cope with. My relationship with my women "bosses" was always more of a partnership, where mutual respect and the breadth of competence offered by our combined talents were hallmarks of our times together. As a teacher, supervisor, and mentor, I had many years to learn how best to guide both men and women. What worked for one gender did not necessarily work for the other. Through the decades, I acquired a great deal of life experience in this regard.

No matter how comprehensive my experiences have been, obviously, as a man, I can never experience what it is like to be a woman. Only a woman can know from the inside what it is like to be a woman. But I can know women from a different perspective: from the outside. And that different perspective can provide information and insight not available from the inside. Of course, the reverse is true as well. Women can see men from a perspective not available to the men themselves, as any woman knows all too well. Together, though, I believe we can obtain a more complete knowing of ourselves and each other than we can in isolation from one another. So I hope the reader will permit my perspective on the feminine, a perspective that I offer from love and respect.

My spiritual teaching comes from that outside-looking-in perspective. When I examined the available spiritual literature, the perspective of a man looking at the spiritual development of women was not well represented, nor was there critical assessment of the inherent gender bias contained in traditional spiritual teachings. This book is my humble offering to begin to fill that gap.

> **Seeker Story**
>
> I met with Richard some years back to get advice on a business venture. As the conversation progressed, I increasingly felt his depth and sensed an intuition that our time together was not merely a "business" meeting. There was something deeper going on. Not long after, a girlfriend and I asked to sit in meditation with Richard because we realized something very special was happening with him. In due course, a women's circle formed around Richard. Now that may sound strange, a man leading a woman's spiritual group, but I believe it's divinely inspired. He is so solid in the world as a man, and as a man of God in deep spiritual connection, he creates a container where women can truly open to their full feminine divinity, their "Goddess" nature.

Women and Men in Partnership

Today, humanity is in the midst of a profound and growing revolution in the relationship between men and women, and as a result mistrust between the genders has increased in certain circles. This is to be expected and accepted. The global initiative for women's rights, like all liberation movements, has caused some necessary friction between the oppressed and the oppressors. But after any revolution must one day come reconciliation, and both factions must again learn to live in harmony. My spiritual work with women is intended to further that newly emerging partnership.

We also can take a lesson from the animal kingdom. Among most mammals, it is rare for the males to have much to do with child-rearing. In fact, in some mammalian species, males are dangerous to young who have not been sired by them. But we humans are rather different. In our species, fathers take a much more active role in family life. It is clear to many ethnologists that the evolution of our human species would have been impossible without a high degree of cooperation between mates. Human family life is much more similar to that of birds than that of our fellow mammals. The successful rearing of young birds and humans alike requires an extraordinary degree of parental cooperation and support. From my readings in human evolution, I have concluded that over millions of years our genders evolved to thrive together, not separately. Our partnership is, I believe, a profound demonstration of the truth of the saying that a man and woman in partnership are greater than the sum of their individual abilities. Our survival as a species would be impossible without this high degree of cooperation. We need each other.

At this point, I will leave further conversation of the topic of gender evolution and cooperation to the experts in that field and now turn to religion and gender. Notwithstanding the male-female cooperation that is a hallmark of our species, throughout most of the history of spirituality and religion, the sexes have been segregated. Training of adepts was done in separate units or facilities. Specific roles and duties in the broad field of spirituality and religion were apportioned to one sex or another, not shared. Men had their domain, and women had theirs.

Only recently, and principally in the West, has coed training become the norm. For the most part, this has meant that women are now permitted to participate in training assemblies heretofore limited to men. While this has created some problems, not the least of which is unauthorized sexual behavior, most people would agree that this integration has overall been for the good and has resulted in more inclusiveness and diversity of opinion, a decrease in sexual stereotyping, more empowerment of women as legitimate emissaries of the Divine, and more commonality of opinion between men and women.

Yet I have taken a different direction in my work. Later, I'll explain the rationale behind my approach to create and teach a spiritual path specifically tailored to women.

Historical Diminishment of the Feminine

It has been a long, long time since the feminine has been properly honored and respected in human culture. For several thousand years, most cultures around the world have had a patriarchal system. First, let's be clear about that definition. *Patriarchy* comes from the Greek. It is a social system in which males are the privileged authority figures over women and children. Men hold the power of political leadership, moral authority, and ownership of property.

For more than a century in Western nations, and to a lesser degree elsewhere, this system and the misogyny it foments has rightly come under criticism, and the roles and rights of women have expanded in these countries, with much more needed progress yet to come. But in a strange and perverse way, that progress for women has come at the expense of the feminine, rather than in support of it.

The women's movement began as a struggle for women's civil rights. In that regard, it made great progress in the last half of the 20th century. Although the revolt against male entitlement was long overdue, it sometimes exhibited an antagonistic stance toward the feminine and womanhood in general. In an era when femininity was treated with contempt and only men had certain rights and privileges, women naturally wanted those rights as well. They wanted the freedom that men possessed, and that hunger also meant that they wished to be freed from the prison of "women's roles" in which they were confined. But within that confinement also lived much of the feminine aspects of a woman's character, and in throwing off those limitations, some of her true femininity was also tossed aside while she embraced aspects of the masculine previously denied her.

For some, the protest expanded to be not only against the culture of patriarchy but also against nature's design for women's reproductive role. If you read the writings of some of the leaders of that era, you find an antipathy toward the feminine and a desire for freedom not only from unfair, biased cultural restrictions but also from her biological heritage: her hormonal cycle, pregnancy, and child-care instincts, for example. Many young women forsook their feminine nature in their quest to "be liberated" and, in so doing, often lost touch with their true essence.

Another great force was (and is) empowering women but also diminishing the feminine during our lifetimes: economic opportunity. More than ever, women are able to free themselves from dependence on a man's income and fund their own lives. This economic independence has been a great liberator. As single-mom and two-earner households became more prevalent, however, this same economic system compelled many women to enter the money economy, whether they wanted to or not. The system of commerce is designed around left-brain, masculine ways of thinking and behaving. Business, like politics, is competitive, even warlike, and the name of the game is to win at all costs, regardless of casualties. It can be a brutish endeavor. Yes, women could now participate with men in the money economy, but they would have to do so on men's terms. That system would not accommodate itself to the feminine. No, she would have to adapt to it if she wanted to participate successfully.

Seeker Story

Becoming a mother was a rite of passage that I initially viewed as disempowering. For many years my identity was based in my career, a very masculine, take-no-prisoners-only-results-matter kind of job. Then, at the age of 35 during the economic downturn, I lost my job, became a wife and mother to a baby and stepmother to a teenager. One day I was gainfully employed in my career and three months later I was recovering from major post-partum complications, caring for a newborn and feeling unprepared emotionally to meet the challenges of womanhood.

Over the course of the next few years while working with the other women in this group, I began to experience an inner blossoming within my being that has super-charged and transformed the life of my family. I liken this experience to a flowering of my womanhood. But it took a while for me to recognize this—that my feminine side had been neglected. I love being reunited with her.

Where I had previously experienced resentment about the exhausting duties of a mother, I now feel pride when I cook, clean and care for those I love. I enjoy caring for my family's home as I infuse it with love. I know my loved ones feel the difference, and I now feel that my love is the greatest gift I can give to my family and the world. I feel secure in my womanhood, proud of my femininity and am open to loving in a way I never dreamed possible. And, oh yes, my career is also doing better than ever, now that it is endowed with my feminine power and presence.

In my career as a business executive and management advisor, I had the opportunity to meet and collaborate with many women who were successful in making this adaptation. Most of the highly successful ones already had well-developed masculine capabilities, so they could easily take advantage of the new opportunities open to women. I saw many more women, however, who had to torture themselves into overcoming their preponderantly feminine polarity in order to compete and survive in the money economy. This has been to their detriment and to the detriment of us all.

The World Needs the Feminine

The feminine is the energy of life itself, the flow from which all else depends. When the feminine has been dishonored and suppressed, we all suffer from its lack. The world is becoming a more barren and brutal place, and the loss of the feminine is at the heart of this withering of life and ascendency of death.

Truly, this is one of the unacknowledged tragedies of our time: the sacrifice of the feminine in the name of women's liberation and economic growth. Therefore, I am gratified to see younger generations of women who are proudly embracing their femininity, but this time without accepting male domination or a labeling of "weakness" in their character. Indeed, they increasingly recognize the awesome power of the feminine, a power that the patriarchy has tried in vain to suppress and control for the past five millennia.

We all, men and women alike, are starving for the life-giving energy of the feminine. But it is a mostly unconscious hunger, one we are hopelessly trying to satisfy with substitutes, including money and sex. If our world is to live in a more enlightened state, the feminine must be cherished. The feminine must be honored. The feminine must be loved and nurtured and supported and protected until she can again safely blossom in the warmth of the sun.

So these are my assumptions: that we each have a polarity in favor of one essence or another, that both women and men have been encouraged to favor masculine characteristics and diminish feminine ones, and that the feminine is needed to nourish life. Our world needs the enlightening presence of the feminine.

On the path that I teach, I empower women to embrace their feminine and find their power and natural home in that set of characteristics. Most are relieved to hear this and are deeply moved to know that this important aspect of them is honored, wanted, and needed.

Most of us have a pretty clear sense of what masculine power is like. The women who are on the path I teach are demonstrating what feminine power is like. The full extent and nature of how that power will be expressed is still to be discovered, but there is one thing we know for certain: It is the power of love; it is the life force itself moving through you.

Since the particular spiritual path that I teach is designed for women, we'll next take a deeper look at the Divine Essence of the feminine.

2

Personality and Essence

Even before we begin formal spiritual training, the characteristics of our personalities can give us hints as to the nature of the unique and personal Divine Essence that abides in each of us. Let's look at this and see how the Divine may flow through you as an awakened woman.

Virtually all of us, almost all of the time, are engaged in some sort of self-improvement project. Maybe you are trying to drop a few pounds or eat a more healthy diet; maybe you are learning something new — a language or a skill; maybe you are trying to be "nicer" to those around you or be more considerate to your spouse or children. We never seem to be satisfied with ourselves, and our imagination never seems to run out of ways we could be better.

Those self-improvements are ideas generated by our egos. In the next chapter, we will see how spiritual growth means listening to something other than the ego. Our ego-based attempts to get better than we are today consume a lot of energy and time. We will need to repurpose that energy and time for our spiritual work.

Therefore, one of the first things I ask my students to do is cease all of their self-improvement efforts. Stop trying to be better. Of course, this raises a lot of consternation. Few of us want to face who we are now, with no prospects of bettering that situation. For example, how would you feel if you were told that you will always have the job you hold today, and your wages will never go up? This is it. No more. That would be a tough pill for any of us to swallow. Or what about "You'll never weigh less than you do now" or "This is as good as it is going to get with your partner?"

In our society, we seem able to tolerate the present only by imagining a better future, but if all prospects for a better future were to evaporate, how would we cope? When I ask my students to cease all efforts at self-improvement, this is the kind of concern that comes up. Let's be clear, however. I'm not condemning them to a life of no betterment. I'm simply asking them to set aside for now any self-improvement projects and turn their efforts elsewhere.

This exercise forces people to look at themselves, at who they are now. When all of our attention is on who we might become someday, we never have to really face who we are now. But if we are going to set off on a journey of discovery, we had better first assess who we are in this present moment and our capabilities to embark on the spiritual journey of discovery.

At some point, my students get past their initial discomfort and take stock of themselves. The next step for the student, then, is to accept the person you are now. I accept you as you are and the other students accept you as you are now, so can you accept yourself? Can you be okay with yourself with all your shortcomings and incomplete development? Because if you can, that acceptance will liberate a tremendous amount of energy and attention for your spiritual journey.

Just loving yourself as you are is a tremendous gift you can give to yourself. No one is perfect, so let's just relax into who we are. All those fanciful projects that your ego thinks up won't be of much benefit anyway, even if you could see them through, which most of the time you don't. Let's turn our attention to what can truly benefit us.

Transformation vs. Improvement

We'll begin by looking at a couple of definitions.

Improve: *To enhance, bring into a better condition*

Transform: *To change in composition, appearance, or structure; to change in nature or character, transmute*

Spiritual awakening is transformation, not improvement. Lots of skills in life involve improvement, which is a matter of degree. Skiing, singing, playing the bagpipes, painting a portrait, algebra, and yodeling all involve skills that build over time. Spiritual awakening is different; it is a transformation of your being. That is a different outcome from improving some aspect of you.

A spiritual teacher is not trying to "fix" you or "heal" you or "improve" you. Rather, we are trying to liberate you from your ego-bound identity. Merely giving you a "better" ego-bound identity is not our role. We are not therapists; we are not motivators in the human potential movement; we do not build up your self-esteem. Our role is very different. It is unique: to return you to your deeper identity, to your essence, to your Divine nature. We do not care if you become a more effective caterpillar; no, we are here to expedite your metamorphosis into a butterfly. So, as regards those betterment projects you are driven to do, give it a rest and instead turn your energy and intention to the liberation your teacher is offering.

Personality Reveals Essence

All humans have distinct personalities, and each personality will have tendencies to react in certain ways. Some tendencies are inherent in our being; whereas, others are learned from our experiences and environment. In this section, we will focus on the innate tendencies of our personality. For example, in response to a threat, an animal (including a human) can flee, fight, or freeze. Each of us has an intrinsic dominant tendency in that regard. Or as another example, some humans are very curious while others are very wary.

In my teaching experience, I have found that certain of these tendencies have a very deep source: our True Self, or what some may call our "soul nature." This source is much deeper than the ego personality and is present at the moment of our birth, if not before. Consequently, if we can work directly with this deeper nature, we may be able to achieve much faster spiritual progress than we could if we worked only with the shallow ego personality and its learned behaviors.

Many scholars in both modern and ancient times have attempted to place personalities into categories or types. Some schemes deal only with the surface personality while others try to reveal more fundamental natures. Of course, humans are very complex, and each of us is unique. Nevertheless, we can at times gain some insight from this way of looking at human behavior. Over the years, I have come across a number of such systems. While I do not fully subscribe to any particular one, the existence of these classification attempts encouraged my exploration as to whether any useful categories could be deduced from the students who came to me. Over time, I came up with a schema that I believe can be very helpful to women spiritual seekers.

Our True Self carries a distinct personal essence or nature. The moment we individuate from the Eternal Unity, the great Oneness, we gain a "color" so to speak, or "flavor," that is uniquely ours. We carry this essence through our lifetime or, as some believe, through many, many lifetimes. As that essence flows through us, its uniqueness shows up in our actions and decisions. This personal "chip off the old Godhead" is what I mean by True Self. Or call it Soul Nature, if you prefer. Other traditions call it our karmic endowment.

If we think of the True Self or Soul Nature as an intermediate step between our pure Divine Essence and our human personality, then it would be reasonable to assume that the particular essence (color, flavor) of our True Self would be reflected in the surface personality. This continuity would offer hints as to how the Divine Essence is channeled through a person.

Every person's ego personality has both good and bad aspects: "He's brilliant but lazy"; "She's talented but arrogant", and so on. We see these tendencies in ourselves, and that is why we are always trying to better ourselves through our self-improvement projects. But as I noted previously, if we want to awaken to our Divine Essence, that approach will lead us astray, for there is no end to the improvements we could make to our surface personality.

This "fix me" approach is always focused on what is wrong, inadequate or incomplete with us. But trying to fix the "wrong" aspects will never get us to our perfect (i.e., Divine) self. Thankfully, there is a better way. As I said, the surface personality can reveal something about the nature of our True Self and, ultimately, our Divine Essence. So let us examine that.

When our Divine Nature encounters the reality of this material world at birth and in infancy, it is a fundamental shock to the newborn's system. In short order, the focus of our infant becomes one of survival. Fear becomes the motivating impulse, and the connection with Divine Essence is lost. This "fall from Grace," our loss of communion with the Divine, is shocking and traumatic, and our little one struggles to cope with the loss. In response, each of us adopts a fundamental coping strategy that is survival-oriented and which is based on a fearful, antagonistic, and mistrustful stance with the world. From then on, we attempt to mediate our interactions with our environment through this fundamental strategy. We will examine that next.

Coping Strategies of the Feminine

As infants, we are too inexperienced to be able to skillfully process the avalanche of experiences thrust upon our wide-open psyches, so we come to rely on a fundamental coping strategy. This strategy is the foundation that underlies the day-in-day-out choices we make. Some choices work; some don't. Some are approved of by others; some aren't. These everyday choices cover every aspect of life and, on the surface, each choice may seem to be independent of the other responses we have to life. If we look carefully, however, we can see that there is a common theme at play beneath the surface, a kind of current that flows through our life.

If we can identify that theme, we will have a much more insightful perspective on our nature than if we are frantically chasing the surface choices and responses we are constantly making. In my work with students, I always try to discover these deeper constancies. While every person is unique, I nevertheless have formulated a typology that seems to serve the students as they reflect on their actions in life.

My schema is not so bold as to proclaim that it captures "types" of women. Rather, I merely posit that there are fundamental coping strategies of the feminine. I'll describe each in turn. Here are the names I have given to each type:

1. Superego (the Inward-Looking Critic)
2. Victim
3. Resistance Fighter (the Rebel)
4. Wrathful Judge (the Outward-looking Critic)
5. Chameleon (the Fraud/Imposter)
6. Give-to-Get (the Manipulator)
7. Accumulator

Each is a negative stance toward life, and each posture arose from the fearful, infantile conclusions that we made about why we were suffering. However, each type also reveals something about our True Self's soul nature. Therefore, in my spiritual training we do not focus on "fixing" this fundamental aspect of our personality. We don't try to make the meek bold or the chatty silent. Instead, we inquire into that dominant tendency to discover how your nature is expressed at the level of your True Self, where love—not fear—prevails. We do not fix or repair or improve that personality strategy; rather, we go through a process of transformation to arrive at our True Self, discovering how that strategy reflects our Divine Essence. It is that very Essence of Love that was with us at our birth, before the traumatic impact with life caused us to forget that purity. We'll discuss the transformation for each of these types, but first, a bit of description of each.

Superego

For an individual of this type, the fundamental conclusion as an infant was "I am bad." As such, the problems and pain she encounters are her fault. Her fundamental self-reference is self-condemnation, and her ego becomes a relentless, unsatisfiable tyrant over her. She can't do anything right.

Victim

The fundamental conclusion as an infant is that life is inherently about suffering, and the self-assessment is that she is helpless and weak and has no control over her life. Throughout life, she tends to be indecisive, lonely, and needy. "Please save me" is the underlying cry.

Resistance Fighter

Rather than succumbing to the oppression of life as does the victim, the resistance fighter rebels. She believes that if she is to survive she must fight back against a world that wants to oppress her. Her fundamental stance in life is opposition. She is a "No!" She is defiant, wants her way, and is willful. However, she is not really seeking freedom. She is seeking freedom *from*, from whatever...fill in the blank.

Wrathful Judge

The wrathful judge has decided that life is "wrong," that it is the source of her suffering and is therefore flawed and must be improved. This critic-of-all-things acts as if she has the wisdom and authority to judge all matters (whether or not anyone else accepts that authority). She lives with restless discontent, as well as anger, or even hatred, over the state of the world and everyone in it. Her ego has become the angry god, and her fundamental experience is dissatisfaction. This constant judging separates her from the imperfect world around her, and this walling-off helps her maintain her own "rightness" and sense of integrity in a polluted world.

Chameleon

The chameleon experiences early on in life that she is nothing. Since she is not seen, she believes she does not exist. Therefore she concludes, "I have to be whatever you want me to be; your desires define me." She is a pleaser. She can be whatever others want and is a mirror for others' desires. If she can please others by performing in this way, they will (she hopes) not hurt or abandon her and instead accept her.

Give to Get
The manipulator has concluded that no one values her; she is worthless. Therefore she has to offer something that others want. This is the "commerce" orientation to life. If she is to survive in such a world, she has to provide something that is valued. Everything comes at a price, so she must become a skillful trader and barterer in order to get by.

Accumulator
The accumulator feels that something is missing in her. She feels empty. The separation from Spirit that birth entails created a void in her that she is always trying to fill. She seeks relief through food, love, material possessions, sex, attention, or other "fillers," or she tries to escape the feeling of emptiness through drugs, alcohol, adventures, and so forth.

Hints of Essence

This can be a depressing list to read. However, we have to face such realities if we are to transform our existence. We have all had a traumatic encounter with life. Even if you feel confident, competent, and happy with your lot, if you probe beneath the surface of your life, I believe you will find a survivalist of one form or another in your ego structure. It is the inherent nature of the ego to have a fearful stance against life. The list outlines the different strategies that women can apply in the face of that fear.

When women read this list, usually one or perhaps two of these strategies jump out as theirs. Yes, we can find a bit of each of the seven working in us at times, but there is likely to be a dominant theme that you fall back on when things get tough.

My students and I have found this schema very useful in exploring patterns of response to life and the world. There are, of course, other available schema you can use. For example, the Enneagram developed by spiritual teachers in the last century, posited nine (or 27) personality types, and the Myers-Briggs personality categorization outlines 16 combinations. Here, I state only that the seven types of my schema show fear-based survival strategies of the feminine personality.

It is important to note that these seven strategies, even though they seem negative, are not aspects of you that have to be "fixed." As part of your essential nature, they can't be "fixed," but they can be transformed from being fear-based to being love-based.

Each of these strategies has its distinct energy signature or tone. Each vibrates a unique essential "song" of creation. In the ego, since its orientation is survival, these songs of creation get transmuted into strategies of survival. Gold into lead, as it were. But the purity of the gold is still there, beneath the surface, and our spiritual work is to uncover that essential purity. It will be the same song, the same energy, the same notes, but played at a higher octave. By following the notes up through the octaves, we will discover how our fundamental energy is expressed at the level of our True Self leading to, ultimately, our Divine Nature.

In the paragraphs that follow I discuss how each survival strategy transforms into an expression of our unique Divine Essence. As you read it, try to feel in your body and heart the energy signature of each personality strategy and then try to feel how that same energy transforms when you read the Divine counterpart.

This is the path of transformation. Instead of having to undergo an arduous, never-ending path of self-improvement projects, we can just make a small adjustment to our vibration, to our personal song, and it will transform from personality to essence. We can do this because our Divine Essence is already within us. It is not something that has to be found elsewhere or developed through practice. It already is. It will feel like a truth you have always known about yourself but somehow forgot. So relax and find the song of your Divine Essence. Watch yourself rise Phoenix-like from the ashes of these personality traits into the flight of the golden one, the Goddess as You.

Here are the strategies and their transformations. (I've changed the sequence of presentation for best effect.)

From Resistance Fighter to Enthusiast

The Resistance Fighter experiences life as energy. From a fear-based egoic perspective, the energy emanating from all those around her must be resisted, and a defensive "no" posture is taken against life as she attempts to become invincible against the world. But what happens if the fear is removed?

At the level of the True Self, love is the reigning emotion, not fear, so she is impelled by the energy of love. When we love something, we are energetically attracted to it and want to approach it. At our deepest level, we have love for everything and everyone, so we are irresistibly attracted to life. The Enthusiast is attracted to life because she is the life force itself, and she sees that life force (herself) everywhere. The Enthusiast exudes a healthy appetite for life and experience and expresses the qualities of spontaneous joy, passion, playful engagement and sexual ecstasy. She is the "Yes!" to Life.

Seeker Story

The transformation of my energy from Resistance Fighter to Enthusiast, from no to yes: I was sitting on the couch across from my dearest friend, former partner, and occasional lover, stuck in one of our usual argumentative loops that go nowhere constructive. I was deep into years of Richard's teachings and my heart was beginning to crack open. I had a particular fondness for and likeness to the resistance fighter. Most of my life energy has been spent fighting for my needs to get met, or fighting to get out from under someone else's "control." I was now beginning to see how at every turn I was sabotaging my own desires by falling into an old pattern of resisting—even when what my soul needed was right in front of me. I was becoming painfully aware that my habit to energetically resist was destroying any chance of happiness that was coming my way.

I sat on that couch and listened to this loving man describe for me what it has been like for him. Why our attempts at relationship always fizzled out. How he never actually felt I was ever giving him 100 percent of me. And I suddenly knew he was right. I was continually holding back those parts of me that my resistance fighter was going to protect at any cost—my whole self, my pain and unworthiness, my fear and vulnerability. It was one of the light-bulb moments where everything became very still and very clear. I closed my eyes and just said one word...yes. And life and love became very simple.

From Chameleon to Empath

The Chameleon experiences life as relationship, but she experiences this through the self-judgment that she is nothing. Therefore if she wants love, approval, or acceptance, she has to become whatever those around her want her to be. She has to perform the desired role. A person can only pull off this deception if she has great skill in reading others. She can do this because she is naturally attuned to others and lives in a continuous flow of energy exchange with everyone around her.

At the level of True Self, when the fear is removed, that attunement can realize its full potential as an expression of love. The ability to "get" the other person is a gift that she can express as compassion and communion. She can also experience the rapture of merging. She can truly say, "I AM connection."

From Give-to-Get to Sacred Service

The woman who believes she is worthless and without value knows she must give something in order to get. Everything comes at a price. She must trade something in order to receive. This is tragic, because this person was born with a capable skill in providing, plus a strong sense of selfless devotion. As such, she is naturally oriented to the needs of others. However, this high state is difficult for the new ego to maintain when faced with the fear of survival. When she believes that her needs will not be met, she must fend for herself and quash her natural yearning to freely give, focusing instead on what she must get to satisfy those needs.

At the level of True Self in its domain of love, her desire to till the garden of love can again flower. She can express her devotion and at last experience profound joy in her service. Her generosity of care nourishes those around her to bloom and thrive, which is all she truly cares about. Their joy is her joy. Every mother experiences some of this, but in this woman, it reaches its full potential. She is the world's gardener.

From Victim to Acceptance

The victim suffers in her helplessness and weakness. However, the source of this suffering is not from the circumstances she is in but from resistance to those circumstances. The suffering arises from her will and desires being unfulfilled. When victims are born, they can actually be far along the path of spiritual awakening.

Surrender is a profound spiritual state, one reached by all the great masters. They understand that desire and aversion are the source of suffering, and if the victim is to escape that human predicament, she must be able to accept what is so as it is. This is the state of equanimity and acceptance referred to in sacred texts. When the victim stops resisting reality, she can reach a kind of holy freedom that the ego cannot comprehend. When she lives surrendered in acceptance, she lives in peace, faith, and trust, and her love is free to flow. In full surrender, there is no such thing as a victim.

> **Seeker Story**
> From Victim to Acceptance: Most of my life I've moved through the world as if I was a small girl inside the body of a grown woman. I've felt like a victimized girl who did not get her needs met when she was little. As a result, the world has felt like a very scary place where I was completely alone (and feeling lonely). I felt weak, helpless, and indecisive. I feared making decisions because I didn't know how to deal with the consequences of a decision as an adult would be able to do. Essentially, I was suffering because I was listening to the loudest voice in the room (i.e., in my head), and it insistently repeated that the world was a scary and unsafe place!
>
> As a result of this spiritual work, I've managed to find distance between my thoughts and my actions. Today, instead of living as a small child, I can hear but not be "hooked" by the inner voice that chatters all day with imagined fears and dangerous scenarios. This voice is still loud and persistent, but I'm learning how to let it chatter away without its making decisions about my adult life. I am learning to live in the Acceptance of

WOMAN, GODDESS & SAVIOR

> What Is, rather than in the perceived fear of being a victim. This process of Surrender has been a journey of trust and faith in both my teacher and in the larger spiritual dimensions that are lovingly holding all life and, in fact, holding me. This journey from Victim to Acceptance, from Suffering to Surrendered, has not been easy. But ultimately it is a journey that has helped me discern the illusion (perceived fear) from reality (all is actually well). And within this clarity lie the pearls of deep truth, insight, and wisdom that increasingly arise unexpectedly in different moments, illuminating my path through the darkness into the light of an awakened existence.

From Accumulator to Union

The accumulator was particularly sensitive to the loss of connection with Spirit that happened through birth. She tries to fill this void through futile efforts to accumulate substitutes, none of which fully satisfy the hunger or fill her emptiness.

At the level of True Self when the sense of connection with Spirit is restored, she at last experiences her dream of being filled with the Divine. As she feels her ecstatic union with Spirit, she also becomes filled with all of existence. Separation disappears and she knows that none of us are separate. In fact, she now knows that there is only an unbroken wholeness. Existence is whole, full, and complete.

From Wrathful Judge to the Beholder

The wrathful judge was born with a great ability to see things as they are, but in the face of the ego's fear of survival, that ability to see becomes tainted with judgment. "I am unhappy, my needs are not being met, so all of existence is flawed" is the conclusion reached. The result is a chronic state of dissatisfaction and a never-ending struggle to make the world "right."

When love, not fear, is the ruling emotion, the ability to see without the taint of dissatisfaction is restored, and the judge becomes the Beholder. The Beholder sees existence, the world, life, and all things in it as perfect. Like a warmhearted grandmother looking at her offspring, she looks in wonder and awe at the perfection of it all. All is beloved to her, all is forgiven, all is redeemed. She sees the perfection of creation; she *is* that seeing.

> **Seeker Story**
>
> I have a very Wrathful Judge living in my head! It is one of my most dominant coping strategies. Actually, it's been such an integral part of me for so long that I didn't even see it as a coping dynamic. It is a constantly chattering voice running a dialog about anything in my life that triggers it. It has two distinct manifestations. One is entirely internal, and is typically centered on someone with whom I have an unresolved issue. It could be a coworker that I don't agree with, or my sister who still hasn't returned my call, or my partner who has done something that irritates me. Because I'm also conflict-avoidant and afraid of being rejected or looking stupid for not understanding something, I tend to keep these unresolved issues in my head for a long time where I conduct an obsessive argument with others, offering up various opinions about why I'm in the right or what they need to hear, or what I want them to say to me, etc., etc.! It's awful really. Nowhere in this repetitive monologue am I loving or curious about the other person. Never are they acknowledged as a Beloved.
>
> Its other manifestation is external and occurs in the form of vocalized opinions about how or what someone else should be doing, as if I have the one and only correct answer/approach/solution. To whatever. With a big cringe, I noticed just recently how my Wrathful Judge occurs with my mom, whom I love dearly. She has always been the nurturer and caretaker in our family and is in constant motion with various household chores: planning a menu, preparing

food, organizing clothes, researching activities for us to do as a family. How wonderful, right? Except lately through my Judging Eyes, I've been disdainful toward her. It comes from the Judge's perception that she does too much and never rests, that she does so much the rest of us never have room or need to step in, and I feel irritated with her "servitude." Instead of seeing her as the Beloved Mother who takes such tremendous care of us, thus deserving nothing but my gushing love and gratitude, I am short and critical of her.

The development of my Wrathful Judge has been so progressive over time that it's hard to say when it began exactly. In a way, it doesn't matter. More important is discovering how incessant and pervasive it is. The shift to be in my heart, to genuinely behold and experience my world as Beloved, deserving of nothing but my love and acceptance and support, has required a very deliberate and mindful uncoupling from this voice, like prying a barnacle from a rock amidst the ocean spray.

From the Superego to I Am

Imagine a god creating a world and then coming into that world, but then feeling pain and suffering. It would be natural for that god to conclude that she is flawed, since her creation is flawed so badly that she suffers in it. That is the fate of our poor infant who enters this material world, still bathed in the glory of her perfection, there to meet a harsh existence. She concludes she must be flawed, bad. What a fall from grace!

Such a child is born in a fullness of Being, in the essential oneness of Creation. At the level of True Self, this knowing was never forgotten, but in the ego she became lost in her self-judgments. As she returns to her True Self, however, the perfection is restored and she experiences her wholeness, her essential Unity with all of existence. The Goddess is born. "I am Spirit."

By describing these seven different strategies, I hope I have given you glimpses into the awakened state, and I hope you have been able to identify your signature strategy.

Though I have called these shifts "transformations," that word is not quite accurate, since you have always been this awakened being. Maybe we should call them remembrances, remembering who you truly are and always were. Each of these states is a high, holy place, but each is also threatening to the ego's control over your identity. "If you do this, we are doomed!" the survival-oriented ego will cry.

This is where faith comes in. The longing to be your higher self has always called to you. The spiritual path, then, is to walk with faith and trust until your True Self is reached. Your spiritual teacher already sees your True Self, so let that servant of Spirit guide you through your fears to your true home.

Now that you have a glimpse of your Divine Nature, we'll next take a look at your readiness for deep spiritual work. Any path of spiritual inquiry is intended for people who are emotionally mature and disciplined, so before delving into the awakening process, let's discuss whether there is any preliminary personal developmental work you need to undertake before setting out on your spiritual adventure.

3

Peter Pan World

Many commentators from diverse walks of life and academic disciplines have concluded that humanity is a young species that has evolved only to the point of adolescence. As a species, we have not yet reached adulthood, they believe, and they cite substantial evidence to make their case. From a spiritual teacher's point of view, this condition is glaringly obvious, so let's examine the implications of it for spiritual awakening.

Before individuals can profitably progress to the deeper domains of spiritual development, they typically must first undertake some "remedial" work and come to grips with their immaturities, the aspects of themselves that have not fully developed to adulthood. Regardless of chronological age, all of us have areas in which our development ceased prematurely, causing us to act from a childish place unsuitable for an adult. I have those aspects, you have them, we all have them, and you probably know what yours are.

If this was only a personal problem, it would be difficult enough to work through our undeveloped aspects. That is the domain of psychotherapy, self-help books, and workshops. But the individual "remodeling" work that we each must do on certain aspects of ourselves is made more difficult by the society in which we live. It is like swimming upstream against a strong current.

Like the fictional Neverland, our society is designed to keep people in perpetual childhood. By and large, people do not mature beyond emotional adolescence, and many never even reach that post-childhood level of development. Merely because someone moves from school to a job, from singlehood to marriage and family, does not mean they have matured in the slightest as a result of these changes in form.

This fact—that we are a society stuck in emotional infancy, childhood, or adolescence—is not glaringly obvious because of its pervasiveness. Average is, by definition, considered normal. Sadly, however, careful examination of people's behavior or their responses on psychological tests reveals how few truly mature adults there are. Even people functioning successfully and in positions of high leadership or positions requiring great expertise and intelligence could seldom be called adults.

Therefore, my dear, if you want to become a Goddess, and as a Goddess you want to save the world with your divine wisdom and compassion, well...there may be a few personality issues to address first. Please don't take this too personally. Our entire society, including educational systems, consumerist economy, and mass media, is designed to ensure that the general population remains emotionally needy, unstable, and quick to react without reflection.

As a result, most people are run by their reactive mind, a mind little changed from our ape ancestor days. Many spiritual paths ignore this problem. The spiritual practices that I teach, however, are designed to further both the process of personal maturation and the development of a person's higher spiritual capabilities. In my spiritual teaching work, we do not begin at the lofty heights of philosophy or supernormal powers but with the humbling work of confronting our own childishness and lack of maturity. The individual's existing life with family, career, and community is the training ground for this basic work. We do not go off to the isolation of the mountaintop or monastery or even the meditation mat. No, we look at how we conduct our daily affairs and discuss how we might handle things more maturely.

It takes a measure of courage and humility to begin one's spiritual work at so humble a level. I will want you to work on parts of yourself that you thought had been resolved before you left high school. Spiritual exotica—kriyas, kundalini energies, mystical visualizations, expansions of consciousness, and epiphanies—can come later. First let's find out, can you be honest? Can you keep your word? Can you stick to a task and program? Can you accept instruction? Can you learn? Can you accomplish assigned tasks? Are you willing to be responsible for your actions? When challenged with adversity, can you resist the temptation of childish emotional outbursts or avoidances? Can you govern your dysfunctional obsessive tendencies?

If you cannot, we both will be wasting our time. Many desire, but few have the dedication to work to achieve their desire. The pursuit of spiritual awakening is not a task for the faint of heart. You will need a healthy, well-individuated psychological makeup. Therefore, before heading out on your spiritual adventure, let's first get you in shape for the journey ahead.

Let me interject here an "on the other hand" comment before continuing our theme. Many spiritual aspirants have heard comments such as "Only a few in any generation can awaken" or "It takes thousands of lifetimes before a soul can awaken" or "Fewer people awaken in any given year than reach the summit of Mount Everest." From this viewpoint, spiritual awakening is seen as a superhuman achievement, attainable only by dedicated spiritual Olympians and certainly not something ordinary humans can aspire to or achieve. My dears, nothing could be further from reality. Spiritual awakening is a latent potential in every one of us; it is our birthright, and some would say the purpose for being a human. So when I say you must have dedication and desire, I don't mean the heroic commitment needed to become an Olympic champion. I mean you have to be a mature, fully functioning adult who will apply herself purposefully to the goal of spiritual awakening. You *can* awaken; it is up to you.

So back to the topic of being an adult... In any kind of learning situation, you have to first accept that you do not yet know. Then you have to be willing to be trained, and in that training you will be critiqued. At this point in your life, you probably have a lot of latitude to define yourself as you see fit. For example, you could say to yourself, "Yes, I am a well-functioning adult" or "I am an accomplished meditator." But whether you are working with me or another spiritual teacher, we may be saying to you, "Er...no, you are not." And you will have to be willing to accept our assessment rather than what you tell yourself. To give a personal example from my early adulthood, like the majority of young men I thought I was a very skillful car driver. That is, until I went to racing school and saw what professional racers could do with a car. That was one of my most humbling weeks, and my ego wanted nothing other than to bolt from the scene and reassemble my dignity.

It is the same for all of us when we encounter any profound learning experience. Our desire to learn and advance ourselves has to trump our urge to defend our ego and dignity. This challenge is more difficult in spiritual work. To be an accomplished racer, golfer, computer programmer, or dancer involves a specific activity, a skill we are adding to our personal inventory. Yes, most of us can submit to learning in such occasions. But spiritual growth is not about adding a new quality or skill; it is about transforming *you*. Spiritual enlightenment is intended to bring about a shift in identity nearly as profound as birth or death.

To make such a dramatic transformation, you will have to be willing to let go of the person you have become and embrace the possibility of a new and greater you. That can be a daunting task for our poor, insecure egos. In a profound way, spiritual awakening means redefining reality itself. This is why all spiritual aspirants are courageous adventurers. They are willing to leave the comfortable confines of the world they know for the hope of something truer and greater, which has been nagging at them from within. That longing or restlessness compels them to embrace the unknown for the chance, even if it is a slim chance, of discovering what has been calling to them. One cannot but admire these daring adventurers for their desire. And it is my great, great privilege to guide them through the unchartered waters to their Promised Land.

Oftentimes people will enter a spiritual path because they are wounded or because life has not been a satisfying endeavor for them. That can be problematic. A spiritual teacher is not a therapist. If you are dealing with serious personal issues, I and many other adepts would want you to work with a therapist or comparable counselor to ensure that you have that kind of professional resource available to you before or while engaging in serious spiritual work.

Even though spiritual work involves transcending conventional ego-based identity, there is an odd paradox here because it takes a well-developed ego structure to do the work of surpassing the ego. (We'll go into the why's later in the book.) It will be best if you are psychologically well-developed before engaging in challenging face-to-face work with a spiritual teacher. If you are not, it would perhaps be better to limit your spiritual activities to reading materials and attending audience events, lectures, maybe meditation classes, and so forth. Those activities can be very valuable, and the number of such offerings is vast.

Embracing the Idea of a Vaster You

Imagine that you lived in the early 1800s somewhere in Europe or another continent and decided to emigrate to the Americas. I wonder if we today can imagine such a momentous decision. At that time, it would have meant totally giving up the life you knew and the place you had in your community—your trade, extended family, reputation—everything you had ever known. You'd be giving up all that for some hope, a dream of a better life, with little possibility of turning back. Even today, migrants from destitute or unsafe regions of the world are seeking the same dream.

When we think of spiritual growth, we may think of the benefits that could accrue to us. Yes, there are great rewards, but you may also have to give up much. Perhaps your material life won't have to change dramatically, but your attitudes about that life will surely change. How you see yourself will change. What you value from relationships will change. So, pilgrim, be prepared to let go. The greater "you" that can emerge may be a lot to handle.

We think we want great love. We think we want the presence of the Divine. We think we want inner peace. But I suspect that what most people actually want is just a little more of those qualities than they have now. Would you want so much of those qualities that you would become a Mother Teresa–type of servant of humanity? Do you want to be lifted by Spirit into a new life, or do you just want your present life to be better, more pleasing, or less stressful? If the latter is true for you, it might be best to focus your spiritual activity on meditation, lectures, and books for now, until your spiritual desire burns hotter. Working one-on-one with a spiritual teacher can be an intense and demanding enterprise.

If you work with a teacher to the point at which your inner Divine Nature gets awakened, that Nature will be much less committed than your ego is to having a nice, comfortable, secure life. It will have its own agenda. As spiritual teachers, our job is to awaken that tiger within, not make your life more comfortable. If there is a hunger, a yearning calling you to a greater life of Spirit, then please come to us. But for many people, their interest in spiritual work is much more modest. No shame in that. Any spiritual impulse is better than none.

Other people are more driven, some even desperate for spiritual illumination. They know they *must* proceed down that path. Spirit is calling and they feel they have no choice but to respond. It is such people who will most benefit from active, face-to-face teaching. For a spiritual teacher, for any coach or teacher really, there is nothing more endearing than an avid student. We want to give ourselves to you and your potential. We are here to serve. So please be prepared to meet us with your mature commitment and dedication.

The following chapters explore spiritual awakening in depth. I hope this book will encourage those who have a true calling for illumination and will help clarify for those who do not, how they may want to proceed with their spiritual inquiry.

PART II

BECOMING A GODDESS

Introduction to Part II

When a woman awakens to her Divine Essence, she becomes a blessing to the world. In this part of the book, we will explore the awakened condition and the path of transformation that leads to that domain.

Many people are content to live conventional lives, but a few restless souls hunger to realize their full potential as a great Being. For such a woman, the greatest gift she can offer to life is to open to the full measure of unconditional Divine Love and service that abide in her sacred center and await awakening. The Divine Essence within each of us does not want to be bound by our fears, social conventions, or strategic, survival-motivated manipulations. The inner Divinity wants to move freely through us, without our shallow thoughts and emotions restricting its flow. Yet for all its power, this Divine energy cannot move unless we allow it. Yes, we can and do confine God. Ultimately, we humans have a daunting choice: to imprison God within and shackle the energy of the Divine, or to open beyond our social and psychological constraints and allow the river of Divine Love to flow and uniquely express itself through us. The great opportunity and challenge of being human is to thusly open to the Divine.

The nature of the Divine Feminine is this: She is the source of unlimited love and the fountain of energy that powers all life. Woman is the connection to the Earth, and she must be honored for this capacity, for if her connection with the Earth is blocked, both our planet's life field and humanity suffer. Woman's call and challenge is to open her heart and allow love to flow freely and fearlessly, to shower the world with her light and bring forth the energy of Divine Love into life and animate it beneficently. Such a spiritually awakened woman transcends her egoic limitations and becomes a true Goddess, bestowing her blessings on the world. She may express this as Venus/Aphrodite or the Great Mother, the Universal Healer or the Priestess, the Sacred Servant or another of the many archetypal forms of the Goddess. In all cases, however, her only desire and passion is to nurture life. Her identity as a separate human is transformed and she becomes all life. She transcends merely doing good works and becomes the flow of love itself. She becomes one with all of existence.

In today's world, however, almost all women live in a state of chronic contraction of their natural feminine radiance. Many live in fear of the overly aggressive male. Others suffer from resentment and anger in response to centuries of male crudity, cruelty, arrogance, and selfishness. In addition, survival in today's society demands that women must expend much effort to develop their masculine side. The result is that the world is starving for the energy of the life-giving feminine, the Divine Feminine, the Goddess in all her forms. Without Her Love, our world is becoming more brutish and barren, a lifeless place. Our world desperately needs the return of the Goddess.

If you feel the call of the Divine, then please read on.

4

The Spiritual Path

Many, many people are interested in spirituality these days. That interest spans a broad range of expressions, from someone who may read a few books on the topic to those who dedicate their lives to serving the divine. Notwithstanding the prevalence of the word "spirituality" in our culture today, the term is a recent addition to common language. Until around a half-century ago, a person was either religious or they weren't. There was no place in society for someone to express their yearning for the divine unless they were in a sanctioned religion. In other words, religions held a monopoly on the god business. Individuals could not chart their own course to the divine nor deign to communicate directly with deities without the intersession of religious authorities.

But today we live in a secular form of society wherein each person is entitled to pursue their religious or spiritual aspirations however they please. While many religious traditionalists may decry this change and feel it is a symptom of societal decline, others argue that this change is for the better. I want to point out one clear improvement: Whatever people's interest in spiritual and religious matters may be, they can now follow that interest according to their own choice and initiative. There is no official state coercion that requires participation in this domain. Whether individuals are doing a little or a lot in their spiritual life, it is because they are choosing to do so, and that authenticity brings a deeper meaning to all concerned.

What do I mean by being on a spiritual path? Being on a path implies a greater obligation and continuity of effort than merely being interested in something. Having a job is a greater duty than a hobby. A marriage is a bigger responsibility than a date. Being on a sports team is a bigger commitment than playing whenever you want. People can have as much spiritual interest as they wish, but to be on a "path" implies a greater obligation and typically includes having an instructor who directs your participation. Also, if you are on a path, your commitment will need to endure over time. Success in any learned endeavor requires practice and study, and a spiritual path is no exception. A spiritual teacher offers information and a structured series of practices that are intended over time to open you to various experiences of an ever-deepening nature that enable you to obtain a greater grasp of true reality. Beliefs carry little importance on such a spiritual path.

But a path to what, exactly? In my teaching, the path is intended to lead to enlightenment. From the perspective of an enlightened person, conventional egocentric existence is seen as a kind of delusional or dreamlike state. Yet for 99.9 percent of the population, that state is known as "normal" life. The purpose of the spiritual path is to awaken from that myopic trance to see existence as it truly is, which is a reality veiled from conventional consciousness.

In this chapter, we'll look at spirituality in its various guises and hopefully help you clarify your level of spiritual desire.

How Spirituality is Different from Religion

These days, we often hear the statement "I'm spiritual but not religious." "Spiritual" is an adjective that means pertaining to the Spirit. "Religion" is a noun that encompasses a set of beliefs, often containing ritualistic practices and a moral code of behavior.

Religion is a communal affair that recognizes formal membership, and members qualify by accepting a set of beliefs and committing to follow (more or less) a code of conduct. Since religions hold their beliefs to be ultimate truths, but at the same time require no proof or evidence for their creed, this naturally sets them in an antagonistic position in relation to scholars and scientists whose lives are committed to evidential knowledge. In addition, since humanity has never agreed on a common set of such beliefs, various religions are constantly at odds with each other. Throughout history, those differences have resulted in terrible, violent conflicts. It is no surprise then, that in recent centuries progressive peoples and their governments have embraced secular forms of society and the codification of laws that permit diversity, especially religious diversity.

In contrast, spirituality is more of a private matter, with emphasis on one's inner convictions and experiences. People who say they are spiritual usually devote time to personal exploration through books and other media, workshops and other organized learning experiences, as well as individual practices. They need not belong to any organization or accept any codified creed.

Although there are organized spiritual groups that sometimes call themselves religions, the essence of their work is to assist people in their individual spiritual development. Creed is generally not the centerpiece. We can think of such groups as more akin to educational institutions than temples of ritualistic observance. They understand that beliefs are of little value. What *is* important are a person's experiences beyond the mental and physical realms. How to live is the focus, not what to believe.

In this book, my focus is purely on the spiritual experience, not on religious beliefs.

"Spiritual" Is Popular

The term "spiritual" covers a wide field of activity. Spirituality of one variety or another is very popular and millions are engaged with this topic in some manner. Spirituality is big. An Internet search of this word will produce more than 100 million hits, and an Amazon search for books on this subject will give you around 200,000 titles. These works encompass a vast variety of genres. There is spiritual awakening of the kind that has been taught for thousands of years in schools of enlightenment. However, many of the current crop of books that discuss spiritual growth are merely encouraging us to live a kinder, more considerate, and thoughtful life. I call them "spirituality light." Nevertheless, there is a large audience that benefits from these works. Other books offer advice for how to have a happier or more prosperous life. Still others discuss metaphysical and occult topics: conferring with spirit entities such as angels, fairies, and other discarnate beings, or how to psychically influence people or events. There are books on shamanic practices and witchcraft, on magic and imagined realms of existence, or ones that teach extended human (psychic) capabilities. Note also that "spiritual" and "spirituality" should not be confused with the word "spiritualism," a more specific term meaning the practice of using a medium to communicate with the spirits of the dead.

Lastly, the topics of meditation, qigong, and yoga are also properly considered spiritual practices.

On the path that I teach, we are concerned with enlightenment, the discovery of one's true nature and the attainment of a stable, supra-egoic state of existence. All the other previous topics are not part of my work.

Spirituality vs. Psychology

Spiritual training works with a very different aspect of our being than does psychology, the human potential movement, or self-help workshops and media. All of these other approaches to human development engage with the first two or three levels of our being and are focused on bringing the individual into greater harmony and more effective functioning within herself and with her environment. These goals are also the focus of various other therapeutic disciplines; however, spiritual growth has different objectives.

Spirituality, as just noted, has as its goal awakening us to the dormant, deeper levels of our being. It is not focused on improving the more conventional, surface aspects of our lives, although such betterment can often occur as a side benefit of spiritual inquiry.

Meditation and yoga are good examples of practices that were originally intended to open an individual to her deeper levels but are now widely used by other fields to improve the quality of life at our surface levels. For example, yoga is offered as a physical fitness practice and meditation is offered for relaxation and calming. Therapists, fitness coaches, and the human potential and self-help industries have readily adopted such spiritual practices, even if the deeper meanings and potentials did not survive the transfer to these other fields.

Psychologists and other therapists are not formally trained in spiritual awakening, and spiritual teachers are often uneducated about the field of psychology. The technology of spiritual awakening and the field of psychology originated and historically developed in very different cultures, with each field, in large measure, ignorant of the developments in the other field. When they finally did meet, there was often dismissive antagonism and professional jealousy.

The field of orthodox psychology did not admit to the existence of the deeper levels of being that are the domain of spiritual practice, and it limited itself to the worldview of scientific materialism. Many spiritual teachers, uneducated about Western psychology, wrongly believed that spiritual development would resolve all of an individual's issues and felt no need for Western-style psychology.

The people who most suffered from this collision of realities were the clients. Psychologists were unequipped to identify or deal effectively with what were, in effect, spiritual crises or influences on their clients from sources not accepted by mainstream science. If a client, for instance, was feeling the effects of an infusion of spiritual energy, the existence of which is denied by Western science, the diagnosis would be that the client was under some sort of delusion, and it would be the alleged delusion that would be treated, not the client's need to adapt to that energy.

With similar arrogance and ignorance, a traditionally trained spiritual teacher would sometimes ignore the psychological difficulties their students were experiencing and attribute a spiritual cause to what were, in actuality, clinical issues, such as bipolar disorder, posttraumatic stress disorder (PTSD), and the like. Spiritual teachers, who often grew up in sheltered communities and may have lived as celibate monks, were ill-prepared to deal with, for example, family therapy matters, child-rearing practices, or the many psychological challenges prevalent in modern society.

Thankfully, progressive therapists and spiritual teachers are both coming to a more respectful acceptance of each other's field and are more likely to defer to the expertise available there, when needed by their clients and students. The growing field of transpersonal psychology is one such example. As more therapists have engaged in their own spiritual explorations, they are using their experiences to better inform their clinical practices. Certain forward-thinking universities have also made great strides in bringing more East-West integration into their psychology programs. In addition, as greater numbers of spiritual teachers are now Western-born and educated, they bring with them their modern knowledge of psychology.

An example of progress in integrating these two fields is the publication of the book, *Spiritual and Religious Competencies in Clinical Practice: Guidelines for Psychotherapists and Mental Health Professionals,* by Cassandra Vieten, PhD, and Shelley Scammell, PsyD. Also notable are the efforts currently under way to add the category of "spiritual emergencies" to the next edition of the American Psychiatric Association's *Diagnostic and Statistical Manual of Mental Disorders* (DSM). Let us hope that psychologists and spiritual teachers will continue to learn from each other's unique and hard-earned gifts.

Not All Spiritual Paths Lead to the Same Enlightenment

Historically, religions and spiritual sects monopolized the culture in which they existed. Their beliefs and practices emerged and grew in isolation from one another. Each institution's writings, rituals, pedagogy, and vocabulary were unique, with little intellectual cross-pollination. Only in recent times and in the "melting pot" of the West have these various traditions been opened to broader public scrutiny and comparison. As a result, many spiritual terms today are widely used in all forms of media and conversation. What were once highly guarded terms with very specific application and meaning are now bandied about in all manner of private and public communications. The terms used by various spiritual traditions, organizations, teachers, and writers are presented in diverse contexts and often with different meanings, and can be used to describe very different conditions.

As with words such as "love," "happiness," "big," or "near," we need to inquire more deeply before we can fully understand the contextual meaning of a word or phrase. One group's "enlightenment" may be very different from another's. In this book, my use of common spiritual terms will be in the broad, general sense that the words are used in public discourse, and not with specific, path-dependent technical meaning, unless I note such application. Similarly, when I use the word "ego" or other psychological terms, I am using them in a general, non-clinical context.

You'll note that I sometimes refer to the "ultimate reality" in theological terms such as the divine, god, spirit, and goddess; whereas, at other times, I might use non-theological expressions such as consciousness, being, the absolute, no-self, and enlightenment. For me, all these words point to the same ultimate cause or state, and I use them interchangeably, depending on which reference will best communicate in the context of that discussion. In the deeper dimensions of reality that can be accessed by a dedicated mystic, the seeming incompatibility between theistic descriptions of the ultimate cause (god) and atheistic descriptions (consciousness) melts away. After all, words are only symbols, and no symbol can capture the felt experience of Oneness. East and West can meet in this dimension. Lastly, please note that I use "awakening" and "enlightenment" synonymously.

This book is not a universally applicable, step-by-step instruction manual for spiritual awakening. Directions for where you want to arrive on a journey depend on where you begin. Getting to London from Chicago is a very different journey than getting there from Liverpool, Nairobi, or Beijing. Each of us is a unique human being situated in unique circumstances, so no one set of directions could possibly apply to everyone.

The travel analogy of one destination is oversimplified, however, since the end goals (the destinations) of various spiritual paths are not identical. So back to the travel analogy, for one group, London may be the destination, for another, Tokyo or Rio. An additional complication arises because each path's roadmap uses different names for their landmarks and destination, so it may take some investigation to discover where a path's ultimate end actually lies, compared with other spiritual paths.

"The" Path or "Your" Path?

One question to ask as you check out various spiritual schools is how much individual attention you will be given and to what extent the practices will be tailored to your specific experience and ability. I find that too many spiritual schools require their students to conform to a very structured or formulaic program of spiritual advancement. And some schools are limited to only a single technique! In my view, people today are far too individuated to benefit efficiently from imposed group programs.

As a former businessman, I understand the "business model" benefits of bringing large groups together under one teacher, where everyone undergoes an identical sourcing. Good for the enterprise, yes, but not such a good use of the students' time or money.

I believe that effective spiritual instruction must be carried out individually and in small groups. Each person's inner world and life history are so unique that personal coaching and attention is essential once a person gets beyond the most basic levels of spiritual exploration. So I recommend you seek out paths that allow for individual counseling combined with small group sessions that will provide customized coaching tailored to your personal needs and abilities.

Spiritual Guidance

I hope you now understand, if you didn't realize it before, that your journey will be unique. Your quest will be an inner one, and since it takes place in your self-constructed inner world, you will be exploring territory no other human has traversed before. Because of this, while books, tapes, and lectures can be helpful, if you are truly serious about spiritual awakening, at some point on your journey you will greatly benefit from an experienced guide. The territory to be explored will, to your ego, possess the characteristics of a wilderness, with all the dangers, confusion, and mystery that word conveys. The territory is wild, the pitfalls real, and the landmarks subtle, so you will want someone you can trust implicitly to coach, encourage, and guide you.

But these days, "spiritual guide services" are a "wild-west, buyer-beware" marketplace. Just as in the mid-1800s when wagon trains were crossing the vast American West to seek new homes for adventurous settlers, today's adventurous spiritual seekers will encounter an array of guides with greatly varying skills, expertise, and motives. You want a guide who can safely lead you to the metaphoric gold fields of California or the fertile acres of Oregon's Willamette Valley, but not to the fate of the Donner party or the uncounted many who perished in the wild rivers and deserts of the American West.

One specific caution: Today we often find spiritual teachers who, like many religious leaders, boldly proclaim that theirs is the one and only true path. My advice, if you hear such a claim, is to run, not walk, to the nearest exit and don't look back. Truly, there are more paths to Spirit than there are clothing selections in a department store. Each of us can find a path that will best fit our aspirations, abilities, and temperament, and no path is suitable for everyone. Your goal as a seeker should be to find the teacher and path that works for you, not the "best" or most famous one in the whole, wide world. Please take the time to explore fully the resources in your community and do your "due diligence" before choosing your guide. Later on, I'll talk more about how to get the most from a relationship with a spiritual teacher.

Enough of the cautionary disclosures; let's move on to the good stuff.

Enlightenment

What is this thing called enlightenment? For many, the word conjures an aura of mystery, a romantic ideal, something beyond the ordinary world: Shangri-La. Hopeful spiritual aspirants believe enlightenment represents a "diploma," which signifies that the aspirant has succeeded, graduated. Descriptions of enlightenment include statements like god absorption, no self, unity consciousness, freedom from mind, and oneness in the ground of being.

Different spiritual paths have different conceptions of what their ultimate outcome is, so no single definition of enlightenment can be made. Due to this and due to the highly inflated use of the word "enlightenment" in general conversation, I prefer to use the less hyperbolic term "awakening." In my usage, the word simply means to live in and operate from a supra-egoic state, that is, not to be confined within the ego-mind and body. Though we may talk about enlightenment as the "awakened state," it is more accurate to think about it as a stage of human evolution and as an ongoing process rather than a final destination or endpoint. In the awakened condition, one continues to experience all the states of consciousness, emotions, and bodily sensations experienced in the unawakened, or unconscious, condition.

In the Introduction, I outlined five levels of our being: acted character, ego, authentic self, true self, and godhead. In conventional consciousness, only our acted character and ego are accessible and known (and our authentic self only rarely), but, with spiritual awakening, all the levels of our being come alive and can be expressed.

Myths about enlightenment and those who have attained it are legion. They tend to portray the enlightened person as a sort of super-hero, perfect in every way and possessed of magical powers. For example, there is the common misconception that after awakening the mind goes blank, and there are no more thoughts. The enlightened being has no ego at all, no feelings, emotions or other personality traits, and the person lives in constant equanimity, abiding in a state of oneness, no matter what is happening. We also tend to believe they have the power of omniscience and clairvoyance. Well, of course none of this is true. Enlightenment is a very normal, natural condition, as we will learn in later chapters.

People who grew up in cultures with belief in an afterlife need to be watchful of the tendency to have enlightenment fill the space of hopefulness and perfection that the notion of Heaven previously occupied, the desire for Heaven being replaced by a desire for the here-on-Earth mythical paradise of enlightenment. Also, many people raised in Western cultures are conditioned to a goal-seeking orientation to life, and they naturally bring that predisposition to their spiritual quest. Even calling it a quest reveals that goal-centric attitude. It would be better and more productive if our efforts were animated by a native curiosity and openness not focused on a specific goal or outcome.

For many people, the desire to pursue spiritual inquiry stems from an emotional source. For some, their motivation is to escape or reduce emotional pain, suffering, and confusion. For such folks, life is not sufficiently satisfying or rewarding, and they are on a search for something that will make it more bearable. They hope spiritual inspiration will be an effective analgesic for their miseries or uncertainties. Other people are animated by a vague sense of longing or hunger, a sense that something is missing. Or they are nagged by the feeling that "this can't be all there is to life." Others feel that something — something undefined and vague, but nevertheless powerful — is stirring in them. Finally, there are those who, like homing pigeons, are instinctively pulled onward by a sense of "home" or "god" calling to them. These emotional hungers and intuitions are what have led people to spiritual exploration throughout history, and we moderns are no different.

If you are one of this tribe, I hope you will find your peace.

Important Distinctions to Know

Duality or nonduality? The first distinction to be made when considering various spiritual paths is the question of duality or nonduality. Duality refers to a subject-object relation between the seeker or believer and the god or gods they seek. In plain English: I am here and the god I seek is somewhere out there, wherever "there" may be; the god(s) and I are separate. Most indigenous religions are primarily dualistic, and their followers worship a variety of gods, from chthonic deities to the spirits of ancestors. Other groups utilize the practice of conferring with some variety of discarnate spirit entities from near and far. All of the Abrahamic religions—Judaism, Christianity, and Islam— are dualistic. Their followers worship a god that is separate from the worshipper. However, each of the Abrahamic religions has spawned offshoots of more mystical sects that believe it is possible to attain oneness with their god: Jewish Kabbalists, the Sufis of Islam (most Western Sufi groups state that they teach a "universal," non-Muslim Sufism), and various Gnostic or other contemplative, mystical sects of Christianity.

According to dualistic belief systems, the deepest level of our being, godhead, is not available. In contrast, nondualistic spirituality has as its goal the attainment of oneness with the god, or if it is a nontheistic (atheistic) spiritual path such as Buddhism, oneness with some ineffable state called by a variety of names: consciousness, being, no-self, or ground unity. Most of the spiritual paths that have come from Asia are nondualistic. I teach a path of nondual awakening. Nondual awakening has no need for intermediary entities such as spirit guides.

Awakening as consciousness, or something more? Many Eastern spiritual paths and traditions guide their students to the awakening of consciousness, sometimes called enlightenment. In

WOMAN, GODDESS & SAVIOR

this state, subject-object relativity disappears and there is only oneness, or onlyness. If viewed theistically, you and god are one; you and all that is are one. It is an indescribable transcendent state beyond distinctions.

Some mystical paths say there is a further state: Once attained and established, the oneness must be brought into the functioning of life itself. It is a state of immanence, or the infusion of the divine into every aspect of life. In addition, there are spiritual paths that teach multiple stages of enlightenment, some up to seven stages, or even more. And other teachers posit several irreducible dimensions of enlightenment.

Of course, in the myriad spiritual paths available these days, there are distinctions within distinctions beyond the basic categories I have outlined here, but that level of detail is not relevant to our conversation. The path that I teach is nondual and addresses both the arising current of spirit (transcendence) and descending current of spirit (immanence). There are further dimensions of the awakening that I teach, which we will examine in the following chapters.

Find Your Way to Your True Self and Your Divinity

Before I lose you completely in the forest of distinctions, however, I want to return to the important message, which is to encourage you to do the work of awakening. The esoteric details of the path or teacher you choose are at this point in your journey of little importance. Find something that speaks to you and commit yourself to it. And if you are not already on a spiritual journey—begin one! The spiritual quest may be the most important work any of us can do in our lifetime. If pursued with commitment, it can transform your life beyond your wildest

65

imagination. Yes, there may also be challenges not anticipated by your wildest imagination, but if you persist through them, the rewards can be enormous, not only for you, but also for everyone you meet. So please, dear sister, discover your Divine Essence and, once found, share her with us. Her presence is so needed in our world.

5

A Man's Path or a Woman's Path?

In ancient times, most societies worshipped a multitude of gods, and many of the gods were assigned the gender of male or female. In those societies, men and women priests and priestesses existed side by side, each with assigned functions and deities to which they attended. Both priestesses and priests had sovereignty in their domain, and their roles and powers were respected by all.

But with the rise of the patriarchy thousands of years ago, men sought a monopoly on the power to confer with and represent the gods. In many societies, priestesses and their goddesses were systematically driven from power. Then, with the advent of the era of "one god only," that god, of course, had to be male and his priests also male. Even today in advanced Western societies, the existence of priestesses can be controversial.

In the Far East also, men claimed to be the supreme holders of the functions of religion and spiritual training, notwithstanding people's continuing veneration of the goddess. Monastic life was almost always restricted to males. This tradition reaches back more than three thousand years. Until the last century or so, women were, for the most part, excluded from spiritual practice and training.

Today, the sciences of physiology and psychology tell us that the brain, nervous system, hormonal systems, and overall makeup of men and women are markedly different. The life motivations, values, and conduct of men and women also display significant differences.

Here is the issue for women who have a spiritual longing they wish to fulfill: Virtually all of the spiritual development paths available today were designed by men, specifically for men. Many of these paths, as I've just noted, have roots that go back thousands of years. Even with a path created by a contemporary guru, the likelihood is that person drew heavily on older, male-oriented traditions to create the "new" path.

[I]t is easier for a woman to feel and be in her body, so she is naturally closer to Being and potentially closer to enlightenment than a man....
— Eckhart Tolle, *The Power of Now*

...women are always pure. They already have all the higher energies in their chakras. They don't have to work and purify themselves the way the men do.
— Llewellyn Vaughan-Lee, quoting Sheikh Bhai Sahib, *The Return of the Feminine and the World Soul*

Though the above quotes illustrate that there are some male adepts who understand that women have a superior capacity for spiritual movement, there are far more teachers who believe women to be inferior in spiritual capacity. Incredibly, there are still some traditional teachers who believe that only men can become enlightened. Even those male teachers who appreciate the unique capabilities of women rarely offer programs specially designed for their female students.

Of course, today there are women spiritual teachers. A distinction must be made, however, between those who were trained in a masculine spiritual tradition and teach from that perspective and those who have resurrected ancient feminine spiritual traditions or who have created genuinely new paths for women, free from excessive masculine influence.

When we look at the modern world, the fact that almost all esoteric spiritual schools available today were originally intended solely for men contains a great irony in the fact that today the majority of spiritual practitioners in Western nations are women. There are millions of women earnestly trying to develop their spiritual depth but doing so in schools originally designed for men. The practice of Yoga, for example, is growing rapidly, with over 70 percent of its participants in the United States being women.

While women comprise the majority of spiritual seekers, almost all Western schools today are coed. Men and women participate on an equal footing with the same practices and lessons. But again, in most schools, whether the teacher is a man or woman, the curriculum is intended for men. These paths contain a great gender bias in favor of the masculine. As this has been the case for many, many lifetimes, however, the existence and extent of that bias and its impact on women is neither understood nor appreciated by the teachers. It's just "the way we've always done things here." When teaching women, these schools may attempt to have the women students "tone down" their feminine characteristics (i.e. emotionalism, heart space, relatedness) and instead hone those masculine traits (i.e. concentration, single-focus, disembodiment) that are deemed essential for spiritual progress.

Nevertheless, many women are succeeding in the traditional, male-oriented spiritual schools. The fact that women can now participate on an equal footing with their male counterparts is a huge achievement, and I do not want to overlook or dismiss the historical significance of this progress. It is an essential phenomenon to help restore gender balance to the world. However, I believe we can and must do better for women who are called to spiritual awakening. Let's discuss that next.

Acceptance of Life

A spiritual path designed for men must successfully address a number of needs peculiar to men. The way that men approach spirituality is but one expression of their overall orientation to life. Men of all eras and societies have a generally uneasy acceptance of life. In later chapters, I'll delve into this in more detail, but for now let me just say that men have great difficulty accepting life as it is. When confronted with a situation, men want to control it, or if that is not possible, avoid it. Life, however, is too chaotic, disordered, and uncontrollable for men to feel comfortable in this world. That dis-ease with life has led men of the modern era to embrace a crusade to control life, to manage it, and make it more "orderly." Men are using science, invention, technology, and organizational design to displace natural systems and replace organic life with a more manufactured and structured life.

In the Far East, men's dis-ease with life led to a different and more religious response: the renunciation of life. The goal of spiritual practice was focused on the effort to transcend life, to leave life behind as much as humanly possible while still living in the body. Ascetic practices were therefore developed to enable the practitioner to transcend the currents, desires, and fluctuations of life in favor of a more eternal, unchanging, fixed state (Samadhi or Nirvana), a state in which all desires, thoughts, and human expression ceased. This negation is the goal of many Eastern spiritualties. You may still need to breathe, drink water, and take in food, but otherwise, you are out of here. (However, certain more secretive tantric sects in Buddhism and Hinduism continued to venerate the female and the senses.)

Thus has life discomfited men. For women, however, their relationship with life is completely different. The feminine *is* life. The feminine is the central current of life; she is the life force itself. Women are more comfortable than men are with the chaos of life and superior in their ability to adapt. For the feminine, it is unthinkable to want to transcend life for some sterile, negated masculine state.

While men of many faiths have diligently pursued the path of negation, a path where the goal is to "purify" themselves of all desire, thought, emotion, and attachment, stripping away everything except absorption in consciousness or god, women's spirituality is very different. While the masculine has an innate yearning for perfection and will undertake heroic efforts to achieve it, the feminine seeks wholeness, a fundamentally different longing. She longs to find unity in the embrace of all existence and in the midst of life itself. As a result, when women have been allowed to practice their own brand of spirituality, their efforts are often designed to bring Spirit down into life and into their own bodies. It is, in some ways, the exact opposite of the masculine path.

While men live more in the conceptual mind, women live more in the body. Consequently, they want to *feel*. And this desire to feel, to emote, to experience is reflected in the growth of Goddess-worshipping sects and in the practices of these women's spiritual paths. Teachers from traditional masculine paths will criticize these feminine-oriented groups along these lines: "They just endlessly talk, feel, and process, perform a ritual or two, and everyone goes home drained and happy. But no one evolves. There is no real spiritual movement happening, no awakening."

Indeed, the critics' point is sometimes valid. Some women's groups do look like this. But it is unfair to apply this criticism to peremptorily dismiss all women's groups. There is a more important point to take from this critique, however, which is that many women are searching for something very different from what traditional, masculine-oriented spiritual paths are offering. We are living in a time of great experimentation by women as they seek to reclaim their spiritual authenticity and power after so many centuries of exclusion and persecution. This desire for something different is also shown by the number of women who are attracted to more indigenous spirituality as practiced by shamans and other traditional practitioners or through the resurrection of previously suppressed Goddess traditions.

All of these approaches—whether traditional masculine-oriented schools, feminine-oriented women's spiritual groups, shamanic schools, or new, innovative experiments—are expressions of the hunger that women have to be united with Spirit. This hunger far exceeds the current spiritual aspirations of men. Therefore, it is essential that spiritual teachers modify their methods to better suit the particular needs of women.

The Path that I Teach

It is this unmet spiritual hunger of women and the mismatch between a tradition-bound field and the needs of modern women that at last called me to teach. Throughout my years as a seeker and adept, I had no desire to be a teacher; however, as the decade of the 2000s rolled into the 2010s the Goddess finally grabbed me by the scruff of my neck and bade me to address this need. So I began to experiment with a select group of women, and the subsequent intimate and intense interplay between me and my students produced the remarkable path of awakening outlined herein.

The path that I teach has grown directly out of my experiences in more than 20 years of spiritual work. While I have had exposure to instruction and transmission from various teachers and have studied extensively the work of other traditions, what I encounter does not become "true" to me until I have personally experienced it. I hope you will apply the same standard to your own spiritual work.

During my years as a seeker and then adept, I saw how women responded to spiritual teachings and noted what moved them forward and what did not. Many discussions with my spiritual sisters gave me additional insights that did not conform to masculine doctrines. Finally, I was blessed to have teachers who respected women and who understood the unacknowledged masculine bias of traditional spiritual paths. When I began to teach on my own, my students confirmed and added to this knowledge base. With their help, I was able to see aspects of awakening that the more traditional paths were unaware of or ignored.

> **Seeker Story**
> During our weekly groups, we sink deeper into Being, and it feels as if an electric force field rises up out of nowhere and surrounds us with a seemingly tangible presence of deep love, compassion, and awakened presence. It is deeply nourishing soul food for my inner being. I could sit in this "container" for hours. My sense is that the Divine Feminine is present in both human form (in our bodies) and in the atmosphere surrounding us, and there is a direct correlation between how present/connected each of us is feeling to the larger power of that collective energy field. Experiencing this is truly a gift. Each of us can be in our own bodies and yet our beings merge in a field of love, support, and fierce tenderness that I have never experienced in any other groups of women, men, or combination of the two.

What I will describe here are the understandings I have come to regarding the nature of spiritual awakening. These were principally formed from my personal encounters with the Divine, with my experiences being rounded out and explained by spiritual texts and teachings. In my journey, I have come to see that awakening has three dimensions, or facets. Each dimension exists in its own right but is inextricably connected to the others. Awakening of one dimension does not automatically mean awakening of the other dimensions. (However, awakening of one dimension can greatly assist in awakening the other two.) I'll give a quick summary of each dimension now and will expand on them in later chapters.

The three dimensions correspond to mind-heart-body or absolute consciousness, love/bliss, and physical existence. Each dimension expresses its own "flavor" or aspect of nondual reality.

While we customarily say "awakening of..." it is more precise to say "awakening of and as..." since when you awaken, you *are* that to which you have awakened.

Awakening of and as Consciousness (Awareness)

Awakening of consciousness is what the majority of the Eastern spiritual paths mean by enlightenment. Consciousness is not the same thing as thinking. Consciousness exists prior to thought and is the ground from which thoughts can arise. Consciousness has a wide variety of meanings and usages but, when used in a spiritual context, it generally refers to the knowing that one "is," that one exists. "I am that I am." While we all have a personal consciousness, that personal consciousness is but one expression of a universal consciousness. This universal consciousness is not a "thing" but, rather, an irreducible aspect of existence. Consciousness is Consciousness. Awakening as consciousness means to know oneself as that and abide in that self-less state.

The primary tool used by most spiritual teachers for this awakening is meditation. Again, meditation has various meanings, but in this case it refers to self-observation of the mind. How we go about the awakening of consciousness on my path is somewhat different, and we will go into that discussion later.

Awakening of and as the Heart (Love)

As consciousness is an irreducible fundamental dimension, so too is love. By "love," I mean *agape*: selfless love, unconditional love. Not love *for* something, as in romantic love, but love without an object, love as a universal force or energy in its own right. This love has none of the sentimentality associated with the egoic love we are accustomed to in romantic and familial relationships. It is a felt state of being that permeates our existence.

Humans experience this love in the heart—not the physical blood pump, but an esoteric heart that seems to reside in that same general location. As we grow deeper in our spiritual practice, we can feel the presence of this Universal Love energy and its animating quality, and increasingly we respond to its call rather than to the selfish demands of our ego.

Virtually all religions have at their core some version of the Golden Rule. Treat others as you would want others to treat you, love selflessly. Spiritual practices to awaken this dimension of the Divine often center on sacred service to others and visualization meditations in which this devotional love is offered to the Divine as well as to others.

Awakening of and as Eros (the Body)

Eros is the life force energy. It animates all living organisms. Sometimes people think of Eros as sexuality, but sexual energy is only one expression of the life force. As used here, Eros is the totality of the life force. Our bodies and minds want to *live*—to move, feel, explore, procreate, eat, relate, experience. So too, there is a fundamental animating force of creation by which the Universe evolves and moves, the impulse to birth the particular out of the unconditioned—Eros as a fundamental quality of existence.

In our lives, we feel separate from all else that exists. I am me; nothing else is me. In this way of thinking, eros is experienced as a very personal force or energy, unique to the individual body. Just as the unawakened person experiences consciousness as a personal attribute, so, too, do we feel that our bodies and life energies are our own.

But our personal eros or life force is but one expression of the universal life force, the one Eros that is an irreducible dimension of reality. As we grow spiritually, we can sense and experience that universal Eros, bring it into harmony with our personal life force, and allow it to overtake our body, cell by cell by cell. Our actual bodies become infused with the Divine. The body itself becomes Holy and of God.

This is a far cry from those Western religions that have long preached that the Spirit is Divine, but the body is profane. In the way that I teach, everything is an expression of the Divine. The awakening of Eros is the true merging of Spirit and matter.

We could visualize these three dimensions of awakening as a circle.

CONSCIOUSNESS/AWARENESS

EROS/EMBODIMENT

HEART/LOVE/AGAPE

In the path that I teach, full awakening takes place only when you have awakened to all three of these dimensions. The ultimate outcome of each of these three facets of awakening is the same: the merging of personal experience and existence with the Universal. Personal love becomes Universal Love. Your consciousness becomes the One Consciousness. Your life force, your eros, becomes one with the Eros of the Universe. Nirvana and Samsara are one. Atman is Brahman.

Beneath the apparent diversity of existence—the plethora of forms that seem to constitute the universe—there is a dimension of oneness, the primordial foundation of existence. Each of the three awakenings opens us to one facet of that unmanifested, uncreated stillness. Different spiritual paths have various names for this esoteric domain. I sometimes call it the Eternal Infinite Oneness (EIO). In this dimension, there is no self and other, no "me" or "it," just the oneness. This domain can be experienced but not spoken or described. Yet it is the "home" that has been calling to us over the ages.

The Interplay of the Dimensions of Awakening

While the three-pronged nature of this path may be an interesting take on awakening, what is most relevant to women is the fact that almost all spiritual paths first focus on the awakening of consciousness. On many spiritual paths, this awakening of consciousness is the end of the journey. Other paths may continue on to bring that awakened state to the living organism; however, the awakening of consciousness is seen as the prerequisite for this further work.

That presumption is not accurate, however. There is no predetermined order in which these dimensions must awaken. Paths designed by men for men always begin with the cultivation of consciousness. Embodiment, if sought at all, comes after the awakening of consciousness. For men, this sequence is natural and also has practical validity. Men have the capacity for savage physical action and an instinctual proclivity for competition and dominance, so before endowing a man's mind and body with more energy and power, teachers want to ensure that the consciousness and moral fiber of the man are great enough and strong enough to express responsibly the tremendous expansion of available power that awakening brings. Therefore, the men must be given austere practices and disciplines to reliably tame those powerful urgings.

For women, however, this is not such an issue, and the natural awakening process is reversed. Their hearts and bodies are already attuned to the Divine, so they can awaken naturally in an embodied way without the societal dangers inherent with the masculine proceeding in this manner. Awakening of the Heart and Eros have a responsive resonance in the feminine. Women can *feel* these dimensions more than they can consciousness. Delving into the Heart and Eros is a natural thing to do for the feminine. Therefore, my path focuses on these two aspects of awakening: the Heart and Eros. In my experience, women can evolve much more rapidly with this focus than when the initial work is aimed at consciousness.

Of course, many, many women have awakened to consciousness and perhaps to further states using traditional male-oriented practices. These women have my admiration and respect. It is my strong belief, however, that many more women would be more greatly motivated in their journey of awakening if spiritual practices were primarily focused on the Heart and Eros.

How my path goes about this, including spiritual practices to further these openings, is the focus of the following chapters.

6

Working with a Spiritual Teacher

Before jumping into the practices that can lead to awakening, let's first discuss how to work productively with a spiritual teacher. In any field of self-improvement, people will typically begin their interest with books and other media, conversations with friends, and the like. As their interest grows, they may participate in large group learning situations: classes, workshops, and retreats. These activities may provide value for a time, but at some point, in order to reach advanced levels of development, they will need hands-on, person-to-person instruction from a master in that field, a personal coach or trainer who can address the unique issues of that person.*

Spiritual development is no different in this regard. Every individual is unique, so no cookie-cutter, standard recipe will suffice. You will want personalized attention. Selecting a teacher is a key decision that will have great consequences for your advancement. You will want to "shop" carefully from the teachers available in your area. Once you have chosen a teacher, let me offer some guidance on how to get the most from that relationship.

When you were young and still in school, was there a particular teacher whom you adored, whose class you couldn't wait to get to, someone who you believed felt you were special and cared personally about you? Let's begin with that feeling. Let yourself be young again; let the years of subsequent armoring and wariness melt away; find your innocence again. Then, when you have selected your guide, bring that feeling state to the spiritual teacher you have chosen. Of course, I'm not advocating that you abandon all intelligent discernment. (Remember my earlier "wild west" caution.) But how about bringing an ante of trust, goodwill, and respect to the table and let that ante build as results come forth through the connection?

The relationship with a true spiritual teacher is very intimate and is both heart-based and knowledge-based (and some would say, soul-based). It is a unique kind of relationship that nevertheless contains aspects of more familiar intimate relationships that a woman might have, such as with father/mother, teacher, mate, mentor, lover, coach, or brother/sister. A spiritual teacher is a guide, motivator, advocate, educator, comforter, challenger, acceptor, and, most important, fearless holder in love of the woman who is seeking enlightenment and the compassionate transmitter and exemplar of that enlightenment.

As with any relationship, the parties must allow time for familiarity, trust, and confidence to build. However, in the same way that in romantic relationships there can be "love at first sight," with instant knowing and bonding between the partners, so too can there be between a seeker and adept a similar sudden knowing that they two are meant to be forever related. But these flashes of divine lightning are infrequent and, whether in romantic or spiritual partnerships, more gradual progress is the norm.

> **Seeker Story**
> I was on a very heavy spiritual path for 15 years, but pulled back when I was in the thick of raising my children. I had been praying to find someone ever since, who could again work with me to break through the layers that kept me from my spiritual depth and truest nature. I've had a few spiritual teachers, and what I have come to know is they are a precious gift. They appear when you are ready for some sort of opening, awakening or transformation in your life. It is as though your soul calls out and miraculously, they appear in front of you. A wise teacher can take a person to their depth, cut through life's distractions, and guide you to the core of who you truly are. Through the presence, teachings, and transmissions received from a spiritual teacher, when matched with a person's desire and commitment, the true nature of your soul can emerge. I know I need that guidance and direction to go deeper within to manifest my destiny.

As most seekers will be inexperienced in spiritual partnership, a novice might encounter misunderstandings, confusions, disappointments, and frustrations in this unique kind of relationship. She may try to relate to the teacher as she would with one of the more familiar intimate relationships noted previously. But that effort will not provide a satisfactory experience since, as I said, while the seeker-teacher relationship may contain some aspects of these other relationships, it also has profound differences from each of them.

Certain other professional relationships also involve intimate openness and vulnerability. For example, a doctor or physical therapist has intimate connection with your body, and a psychologist has intimate access to your mind and emotions. The spiritual teacher has unique intimate communion with your deeper domains of Being and Divine Nature. With any of these relationships, the more the client embraces that intimacy in an open manner, the more effective the relationship will be.

To help guide a prospective seeker, let's take some time to talk about this precious relationship and how it may evolve. A seeker-adept relationship typically progresses through certain phases, which I name:

1. Ears & Eyes
2. The Cushion
3. The Yes
4. The Yoke
5. Partners in Divine Service

As you move to each deeper phase, the impact that a teacher can have on your progress increases dramatically.

The Ear and Eye Phase

You may hear about a teacher from an acquaintance or friend, or find a book (the eye) or talk (the ear) by the teacher. As a result, you are interested. You are curious. You want to investigate more. So you go to listen to them or obtain media, and continue with this as long as your interest persists. In this stage, the teacher's role is to be a motivator, a "sales rep" of the divine. You, in turn, are willing to explore and learn but have made no commitment.

The Cushion Phase

If the ear and eye phase is sufficiently rewarding, you decide you definitely want to receive the teachings of this adept, and so you commit to more in-depth education. If the teaching is meditation-based, you sit on the cushion and do the work. You are hungry for more, come to sessions regularly, and attend longer workshops when you can. Individual consultations may occur and a personal relationship begins to be cultivated. You are enthusiastic, but one foot is still out the door. In this phase, the relationship is very much that of student and teacher. You are steadily learning and are willing to receive input that may be uncomfortable to face.

> **Seeker Story**
> I'm known as the reluctant spiritual seeker of our group. (Even typing these words feels odd!) I came into the group because I loved our teacher and respected him. We had met in a yoga class a few years prior and a loving friendship unfolded. I often joke that I was abducted into our women's group—but that would not be fair. I knew there was something magical here that would help me discover an expanded version of my best self, and oh was I right.
> The women here are fully committed to no longer participating in their own enslavement. It's not for the faint of heart. Our egos have every reason in the world why we don't need to show up next week. I see evidence all around me that those of us who are experiencing the biggest shifts are the ones who are most committed to doing the work. And the biggest support that we have is within our circle. Watching everyone come back week after week—through blood, sweat and tears—is what keeps us all on track, doing our practices. To do this work without a committed group of women would not be possible for me. I not only feel deeply supported by the women who compose the container of our group, I also feel a responsibility for showing up with my sleeves rolled up and my heart undefended because my healing is their healing, and their triumphs in consciousness are my wins as well.

The Yes Phase

At some point, the seeker wants to jump in fully, wants to "join the team" so to speak. She consistently expresses a "yes" to taking direction. This phase has similarities to the relationship of a coach and a player. The player shows up for all practices and enthusiastically follows the orders of the coach. She accepts that she has a responsibility to the team as well as herself and is eager to bear that responsibility. She expects that she will be challenged and stretched. In this phase, a deep bond can develop of mutual love, trust, and respect.

The Yoke Phase

As the seeker progresses to ever-deeper levels of self-realization, at some point her desire to be awakened becomes so powerful that it overshadows what remaining selfish, fearful or mistrustful impulses may still arise from time to time. The seeker has surrendered fully to her leader and is beginning to sense the arising Divinity within her. Personal will and desire have been tamed, and the fire of the Divine burns in her.

A common metaphor used in spiritual traditions is that of the ox pulling the cart of the Divine, dutifully doing the work of Spirit. At this phase the student accepts this "yoke" from the Divine. (The words "yoga" and "yoke" come from the same root, which in this context means to join, link or unite.) The adept who is guiding her to her awakening becomes the wise and venerated sage whom she holds in adoration and devotion, and she, in turn, is held in steadfast love by that transmitter of Divine Light. Their energies have fully aligned in service to her awakening; they are as one being in this pursuit.

> **Seeker Story**
>
> What I have come to know is that my teacher has my best interests at heart. I have gradually learned that the faster I can surrender and let go, the more happens for me spiritually. Every time I sit with my teacher something very magical happens, because with his being and his teachings comes a transmission of energy that is very life changing. The more I open to my teacher the more I change. It took time to realize this, because I needed many positive experiences in order to be able to trust enough to surrender so completely that one is intimately linked and permeable to another.
>
> The teacher's power of love is benevolent and very firm, yet deeply moving and loving. I also know that I make him such a complete gift because it is my openness that supports him in being able to see and guide me from such a very clear and aware vantage point.

Partners in Divine Service

In the deepest expression of their relationship, the inner Divine Presence becomes the guide, slowly replacing the leadership of the adept. "Thy will, not my will" becomes the guiding principle for our seeker, and she wants only to be used fully in sweet service to the Divine. The concept of leader and follower falls away, and they become true partners in service to Spirit. Even more than that, she is not separate from the leader; they have become one being in two bodies. With both of them now true servants of the Light, that Light may have them continue to work together or the Light may direct them to far places in the world to do its work. But however far apart their bodies may be, their hearts will be ever connected.

Your Teacher Is Human

As you can see from this progression, the relationship between a seeker and teacher is a profound partnership, one with mutually deep, loving trust. With the feeling of such love, it is easy to become enamored with your partner. You will no doubt have great respect for your guide, but we should take care that the love and respect not lead to unrealistic expectations. Whenever anyone is placed by another on a pedestal, the inevitable outcome will be a fall.

Elsewhere in the book, I note that, in the fully awakened condition, a person will feel all the emotions and passions that everyone else faces. Your teacher is no exception, so please allow her or him to be human and exhibit the full range of responses to life that all of us have, even if only occasionally. Spiritual literature often adds to the image of "enlightened" people as perfect superheroes. This fairy tale portrayal creates unrealistic expectations that are bound to be disappointed. Though one would hope that an adept would be less vulnerable than regular folks in dealing with his or her shadow side, no one is a perfect saint.

Teaching something as internal and subjective as spiritual awakening is an extraordinarily difficult endeavor. In such complex matters, guidance will be hit or miss, even by the most skilled and experienced teachers. Remember, a teacher's direction doesn't have to be perfect; they just have to be better at it than you. So please cut your teacher some slack.

Finally, let's remind ourselves that great accomplishment in one area of life doesn't necessarily translate into great ability in every area of life. You wouldn't want your local football hero to conduct brain surgery on you or your philosophy professor to advise your investment strategy. Just because someone has "awakened" does not mean they can manage a family budget competently or know the best hotels in Prague. They only know the spiritual path.

Whenever you feel concerned about the guidance you are receiving, please bring your concerns to the teacher. Only in a condition of full communication can love and trust grow. Your teacher is very committed to your success, so be responsible for giving your teacher the feedback she or he needs.

Basking in the Glory of the Great One

People enter spiritual study from a variety of motives. Obviously, the preferred motive is a sincere desire for spiritual realization. As I noted elsewhere, however, there are many other motives that pull people to find a spiritual teacher.

Westerners are very status conscious, and they seek brands they believe will enhance their stature in the eyes of others. That habitual tendency can come into play when searching for a spiritual teacher. The quest to find the most suitable teacher can instead become a search for the most prestigious, highest-status "brand." When we buy any consumer product, people typically have dual motives. First, they want the product to provide some functional purpose. We want an automobile, for example, to get us from here to there. If functionality was our only motive, however, the economy could get by with a fraction of what gets produced. We over-consume because of the second motive: We want the product and brand name to give us status and make us more desirable. This second motive is usually the more important of the two.

The spiritual marketplace is not immune to this consumer brand orientation. Rather than finding a spiritual teacher who is best matched to their needs for spiritual guidance, many people select the most famous, best known, and "greatest of the great" teacher (today's fad). In other words, they want to select the most prestigious brand. For these people, a spiritual teacher fulfills the same need as a designer purse or shoes. The name of the teacher is intended to add stature to the ego of the student.

Most of these individuals have little interest in awakening; they only want to add a little spirituality to their life and exhibit that to their friends. They are seeking to build a "spiritual ego," and want a brand (teacher) who will be recognized and who will elicit oohs and aahs from their friends. We teachers call it "basking in the reflected glory of the teacher."

If you are truly passionate about awakening, do not fall into this temptation. Rather, select an individual teacher you will be able to trust and with whom you can communicate well. Choose someone who will give you individual attention and with whom you feel a deep connection. You are seeking a true partner for your journey, not a "brand" to put on your knapsack.

One of my students told me recently, "I recall my last teacher who I studied with for five years and developed a very deep relationship, saying to me 'People in today's world jump from teacher to teacher looking for something that will make them feel better. While that is fine, and it is important to try out different teachings, eventually, if you're really serious about a spiritual path, you need to find your teacher, stick your butt to them like glue, and don't let go.'"

My wish for everyone is that they find the perfect guide to lead them home.

7

Spiritual Sisters

The founders of religions and spiritual paths have always recognized the importance of community, the spiritual *sangha*. They understood that the aspirations and life practices of spiritually motivated people differ greatly from the materialistic lives of the general population. Therefore, committed spiritual seekers and their teachers tended to segregate themselves from the society in which they lived in order to pursue a more dedicated and focused lifestyle, one freer from distraction and, frankly, worldly temptation.

Today it is not generally possible for spiritual aspirants to retire to the proverbial mountaintop. The great majority of us must pursue our spiritual work in the midst of society. We have jobs, families, and networks of relationships that are important to us, as well as responsibilities we cannot shrug off. When modern spiritual teachers design their paths, they must take this change of historical circumstances into account. They must develop practices that a modern life can accommodate.

The practices I created, for example, were specifically designed with these conditions in mind. They can be effective for the individual to use on her own. A woman's progress can be augmented greatly, however, if she has close connections with other people who are also passionately pursuing their spiritual calling. Ideally, those relationships would be on the same path with the same teacher.

> **Seeker Story**
> It has been an amazing experience to share a common spiritual path and teacher with a solid group of women. There are ways in which I feel like they know me and see me like no one else can. The relationships are so very intimate. And the strength of the group field when we drop in together makes so much possible. It is remarkable how affected we are by one another's growth, how congruent it is at times, and how we heal collectively through sharing the process of the individual.
>
> It isn't always easy—intimate relationships can be confronting—but on this spiritual path we are given the opportunity to use the conflicts that can arise in relationship as opportunities for spiritual growth. It is a unique and beautiful orientation toward life and relationship that serves a higher purpose. We get to experience the radical idea of the possibility of unconditional love.

> **Seeker Story**
> I remember when I realized that this was not an average group of women. It helps to have a male leader, in order to focus our attention, as well as our intentions. Left to our own devices, we would unconsciously play out needs for establishing ourselves in the hierarchy, or just get chatty. Although I have individuals and groups of friends I feel supported by, this group of women has a whole other level of support. We are held in the greater container of waking up, and the capacity for support of each other is immense within this container. We are sisters on a journey together that has an ultimate destination, and the field

> that we enter together is deep and wide. In that field, the normal ways of judging each other against ourselves lose their significance. These women are supporting my true self emerging, not my personality structures.
>
> Even with conflicts I have had with women in the group, they have been held by a larger container. The conflicts have sometimes been an affront to my personality structure, so are an opportunity to not act from regular ego defenses, but to cook in the feelings I have been trying to avoid through the development of ego structures. All of it is fodder for awakening, and with the container of the group, I have been able to burn through some very challenging situations.

Women are communal beings, and it is important for them to have a body of people with whom they can intimately share their lives. It is difficult for someone who is not spiritually inclined to understand fully and be open to communications from a person who is fervent about their spiritual work. It is therefore a great benefit to have close friends who are on the same or similar spiritual path, or if they did not all originate as intimate acquaintances, that they soon get to know each other deeply and develop a bond of love and support.

Because of this, on my path we organize the students into sacred "goddess circles," small teaching groups of women who are at a similar stage on their spiritual journeys. This provides ample space for conversational sharing and emotional support, and also provides polarity balance to my masculine presence. Participation in a circle also builds intimate relationships among the members, which then establishes a foundation for mutual support in all aspects of their lives. Their combined energy can result in a very powerful field of spiritual energy that can propel the members in a way that would not be possible if they were alone in their practices.

> **Seeker Story**
> We meet in circle every week and it has become one of my most cherished and essential activities. It's different than a 1:1 relationship with a spiritual teacher. By sitting in circle with like-minded women who are also focused on their spiritual awakening, three important things have happened. One is simply the experience of being witnessed by others. What this has meant for me is that I can bring the dynamics of my life and my spiritual work to the circle and know it will be listened to and supported and loved by the other women, who I know will be there to hold my hand or give me a hug when things get rough, as well as celebrate the joys in my life. And in turn I'm providing this love and support to each of them.
>
> In addition to being witnessed, being in spiritual community has helped me experience the commonalities that can exist across women as we navigate our respective lives. What lived as solitary feelings and challenges in my head are now shared expressions with other women who struggle with similar things. During various teachings we have received, it's been invaluable to process them with other women. To hear their interpretations and understandings, which often deepen my own, to hold their tears as they pull back another layer, which then draws me into the softer or more deeply buried places in myself.
>
> This sharing has created the third powerful impact of our spiritual sangha, which is a kind of momentum. After three and half years of being in circle with many of the same women, I can look back and see the unfolding progress that each of us has made on our respective journeys. By now, we know each other's hooks and patterns, and we can see them changing. It's like being in the guts of it with each other, "fighting the monsters" until there is freedom from them. And it's happening

> with *all* of us now, like a collective upsurge in both the depth of the work we are each doing, and the simultaneous broadening of our capacities as awakened women. As each woman goes deeper and each woman gets wider in what she can hold, it is drawing the other women to those same depths and heights. We are collectively creating this.

The support of spiritual sisters can be an invaluable aid to your spiritual progress. Their mutual support and assistance can buoy you up when your interest flags. Their trials, tribulations, and triumphs can be inspiring examples of spiritual commitment, and the growing depth of their love for you a true comfort as you face the challenges of spiritual growth.

Every week, I witness this gift that my students give to each other. I hope you will be able to find a similar committed sisterhood on your path. You are each other's most cherished partners.

8

Life, Attention, and the Witness

The best place to begin your journey of awakening is to examine the concept of attention. Life is all about attention. Where your attention goes, there your life is. Unless you are in deep sleep, at every instant in time, your attention is drawn to something. In taking a bath, for example, your attention could first be on the heat of the water on your skin, but then the sound of the splashing water next attracts that ever-restless seeker: attention. A second later, and a thought arises that your report is due the next morning, followed by an idea of what theme will dominate that report. But that reverie is soon interrupted by the itch below your nose, which in turn is replaced by the memory of wiping the sniffles from your child's nose last week. Then the phone rings, and it seizes your attention. And so it goes, moment by moment by moment for an entire lifetime, a progression of instants that never ends. If you just sit quietly for a few minutes and watch where your attention goes, you will see this phenomenon for yourself.

We probably don't think of life in this way, as a never-ending sequence of independent moments, moments that have no elegant flow, logic, or clear cause. No, we normally think of our life as a whole, as something intact that has been built over time into a solid edifice. As we think of our life as an integral whole of experiences and memories, so, too, do we think of ourselves as a continuing, coherent unity, a substantive person unique from all others.

A house is different from a junkyard. Both may contain similar materials and contents, but in a house the items possess order. A house is more than the sum of its parts, and that "more" is its design, its order, and the intention of the intelligence behind it. Similarly, we think of ourselves as a discrete entity possessing order. When we actually look at the flow of our attention, however, it is difficult to find such order, design, or coherency. If we take some time to be still and simply watch the flow of our attention, the experience is more like viewing a television screen that randomly changes channels every few seconds.

This is disturbing to the order-seeking nature of mind. So our tendency is to stay unconscious about this strange anomaly, summed up thusly: It is obvious to people that they exist and that their existence has an implicit design, yet the process by which life shows up moment by moment in our attention seems not to have much design or order; it is more like the junkyard.

If you doubt that attention keeps jumping from topic to topic like a water droplet on a hot skillet, try this exercise: Stop reading now, close your eyes, and put one thing into your attention. It doesn't matter what it is. It could be the image of an elephant, or the feel of your breath through your nose, or listening to a nearby continuing sound. Now, and this is the hard part, do not allow your attention to shift to anything else. Keep focused on only that one object of attention…only on that object. If you try

WOMAN, GODDESS & SAVIOR

this, you will find that it is easier to keep your breath held than it is to keep your attention held.

In addition to the randomness of attention, there is the equally profound and perplexing question: "From what/where do these moments arise?" What causes our attention to focus on this, then that, then something else? If you look closely, it will be clear that the shifts in attention are not following your commands. They just happen.

At what point does a series of letters become a word? At what point does a series of words become a sentence that conveys a meaning beyond the individual words? At what point does a sequence of sentences become a story? And what is the process that allows us to make those leaps? How can a succession of jumbled moments of attention in a life lead to the sense that there is a whole here (me), a being who has a lifelong story unfolding? Who or what creates this meaning? And what is the consequence of having this meaning, the conclusion of which is that there is a "me" who has "my life?"

Now, in the midst of your life's mundane and insistent demands of working, eating, cleaning, communicating, caring for others, and a thousand other to-do's that must be accomplished, these reflections may seem unimportant or even silly. But if not answered, we and our life will forever feel somehow incomplete, and our living will be distorted from fragmentary and false notions. The answers to these questions go to the heart of our humanness…and our Divinity.

Taking a few minutes to watch this flow of attention, just to watch it without judging it or trying to control it and, instead, simply observing the process can be revolutionary. The flow is happening all the time, yet it is never really noticed.

Witnessing the Mind

Many spiritual paths utilize the practice of meditation in order to bring conscious awareness to this ever-evolving play of attention. They do this because, for most people, this dance passes by without notice. Since it is present all the time, its existence fades into background "noise." Adepts throughout history and across cultures have recognized that watchful awareness of the dance of attention is crucial if we are to explore and discover the deeper realities that underlie our existence. Therefore, they offer meditation training, which usually involves putting the student in a quiet room where no distracting activity is taking place, in order to enable students to put their full focus on what their mind is doing, moment by moment by moment.

Initially, this seemingly simple task is very difficult for the novice to sustain. As with any skill, with persistence, the learner can observe the play of attention for longer periods of time. In many spiritual paths, the student is then offered methods to train the mind to keep attention focused on a single thing for extended lengths of time.

In the path that I teach, I do not offer a single specific meditation technique. Most people who are attracted to my work have had experience with other spiritual teachings and have received some training in meditation. So rather than teach the student to observe the play of attention in the artificial environment of meditation, I ask them to observe the workings of their mind in their daily lives. I guide them to be always aware of a part of their being that they probably have not noticed before, the one who is constantly watching the play of attention. If a person is talking on the phone, for example, I ask them not only to be on the call, but also to observe themselves talking and listening on the call. "Notice what you are saying; notice what your body is feeling," I will say.

In this method of "living meditation," I am asking them to be both the participant in their life, doing and thinking whatever they are involved with, as everyone does, but to be also the observer of what they, the participant, are involved in. It is somewhat like being a 24-hour on-duty videographer of what you the subject are doing at every moment in the reality show of your life, and doing this with enough clarity that you could make a report about the participant's activities if you were called to do so.

We call this observer part of ourselves "the witness." It is not there to guide, criticize, judge, comment on, or be involved in any way. It simply notes. Meanwhile, your participant/player/thinker/doer goes on with life as she has always done. And the witness observes it all, including the ego's reactions to being witnessed.

This may seem like an odd thing to do, and perhaps it is. But it is also transformational. We are accustomed to casual observance, watching what other people say and do, so disinterested "witnessing" is natural to us. We just haven't applied that way of being in the world to our own lives. We look out at the world through the lens of our inner observer, but now we focus the observer on the mirror of ourselves.

"I witness me" represents a major step in the evolution of our consciousness and maturity. As humans grow in maturity, they pass through many developmental stages. At some point, for example, an infant can recognize herself in the mirror. At a later age, she can begin to imagine what another person may be thinking about her. Witnessing yourself is a similar developmental step, but one curiously overlooked in most societies. It is a step that every human should take but which in practice is extremely rare.

When you first begin to practice this, it may seem awkward for a while, but you will learn that you can do it. The main issue you will face is that you will forget to witness. When you notice that you have not been witnessing, simply start witnessing again. If you feel frustrated, relax, just give it time. You can walk and chew gum at the same time, and so, too, you will learn this.

As you persist in this witnessing, you will notice that it is impacting your life in many ways, most of them unexpected. Socrates said: *The unexamined life is not worth living*. He may have meant that it is important to reflect on one's life, but in our witnessing practice, we are, in effect, examining our life in real time, moment by moment by moment. You will be amazed at what a gift it is to create space between yourself and your reactive mind.

Seeker Story

For years I wanted a meditation practice because I knew it would be beneficial, but I lacked the time, discipline or focus for anything to really take root, despite my various attempts. I would sit on the cushion and try to watch my breath or notice my thoughts, but mostly I just found it frustrating that my mind was a constant whirl of mostly repetitive planning, thinking, imagining—and sitting to listen to it was less than desirable.

Establishing a relationship with my internal witness has changed everything. Until now, I had absolutely no separation between those thoughts constantly "on" in my head and the bucket of often overwhelming emotions that have pretty much run me most of my life. Mostly I just kept myself busy with work, friends, activity, while occasionally crashing completely

> from emotions or exhaustion, then picking myself up and doing it all over again. Even years of therapy, which certainly helped me better understand the construct of my mental and emotional makeup, hadn't developed my ability to *detach* from them.
>
> Now, with access to an internal observer, I am able to shift from being lost in my thoughts to seeing them as they occur. So amazing! Sometimes I can even laugh at myself and note, "Wow, that was a pretty interesting stream of thought you just had there," and recognize it as my always-on mind.
>
> Establishing a witness consciousness with my emotions has taken more diligent practice. Especially, those hot-spot emotions that hook you almost immediately can take you down. It's really hard to separate from those. But with practice and commitment I can witness when those emotions have taken over, and can say, "Ah, there's that feeling of being not good enough again" or "He really pissed you off, didn't he?" Instead of being lost in emotions for hours or days, now I see them as a pattern of reaction that I have attached a whole narrative of meaning to, and I can move past them quickly. Which of course is shifting my relationships with others and myself.
>
> Increasingly and interestingly, I now actually crave time on the cushion, rather than having to *make* myself sit. The whirl of my heart and mind is slowly being replaced with a stillness that I'm learning is not only vast and quiet, but also deeply nourishing. I am so grateful.

For readers who have had no or little experience with meditation, it may help to first establish some sort of traditional meditative practice before trying my "living meditation" method. There are a multitude of books on meditation, so you are sure to find a method that will suit your needs and temperament. I recommend Adyashanti's *True Meditation*, which details a very effective method, as well as any of the meditation practices that focus on the breath and body, such as Vipassana. But really, practice what you find works for you.

Developing the skill to witness your mind, whether by the living meditation that I teach or by traditional meditative practices, is the first fundamental practice to master on the road to spiritual awakening. We'll look at this topic in more detail in the next chapter.

9

Mastering the Ego

Spiritual paths emphasize the need to transcend the ego and go beyond that limited identity of oneself. Some teachers even say it is necessary to "kill" the ego, but I do not hold to that extreme viewpoint. Nevertheless, a certain degree of mastery over the ego is required.

The ego is sometimes compared to an unruly dog. We've all see people walking their dogs where the dog is the one in charge. The dog is walking the person. One of the initial tasks of spiritual work is to teach the dog (ego) to heel and follow us obediently. This is a tricky business because for most of us, we *are* our ego. There is no "me" and "it" relationship with the ego, there is only "me." Developing the ability to discriminate between the two is the foundation upon which further spiritual development can take place.

This is also tricky because it is the ego that wanted us to investigate spiritual work in the first place. Our ego is always looking for strategies to make us happier. Unless your ego decided that spiritual work could be one avenue for more happiness, you probably wouldn't have picked up this or any other spiritual book.

Let's get clearer about what exactly we mean by "ego."

Meeting Your Committee

You have voices inside your head. (Perhaps one of them just said, "What voices?" Or maybe they are reading this text out loud in your head.) Don't be concerned; we all have these voices. Just take a minute to notice what they are saying now. We may call it thinking, but it is done out loud (in your head) by talking.

When you start paying attention to these voices, the first thing you notice is that they never stop talking. It is a nonstop gabfest. Yakkety yakkety yakkety yak. In virtually every wakeful moment, the voices are there, commenting on everything, revisiting the past, imagining the future, daydreaming, and judging you and everyone else. In large measure, it is those voices that you regard as "me." You are those voices. Just listen to them…

The next thing I'd like you to notice is that it is not one voice but a group of voices, each with its own personality. If you pay attention, you will often hear them arguing. This doesn't mean you are crazy. Again, we all have an unruly mob inside our heads. I call this mob "the committee."

I suggest to my students that they think of the committee in this way: Imagine you are at lunch with a group of friends. They aren't really close friends; they are in your network and you all lunch together from time to time just to stay acquainted. Maybe you went to school with them some years ago, or you used to work in the same company. They are the kind of people who would be gossiping about you if you missed the lunch. At one time you had things in common with them, but you have evolved and moved on, and they are stuck in the past.

That's the kind of group you have inside your head. They are the committee that is managing your life. This is the decision-making "brain trust" that is guiding your destiny. OMG! And as with the friends at lunch, as you observe your committee you find that you are not the one in charge of the conversation. The topics and sequences are not selected and created by you, they just happen. Perhaps you are able to insert your thoughts into the conversation for a few moments, but soon the conversation is off on its own power without your direction. If you watch carefully you will see that the committee is its own entity, separate from you. This is a major discovery. The committee of voices in your head is not you!

An initial step in spiritual development is to create some space between that group and you. You have to awaken from hypnotic absorption in the committee's conversations to find your own separate space of existence. The best analogy I can give for this is being in a movie theater. When you walk into a theater, you are aware that you are coming to watch a film, then the lights dim, the admonishment to turn off your cell phone is made, the coming attractions roll, and the movie begins. For a few short moments, you are aware that you are watching a film, but then something profound happens. Your awareness that you are a separate watcher disappears and you become fully absorbed in the film. You become mesmerized and are now "in" the film, inside its characters, experiencing what they experience. At the same time, you have lost awareness of "you." Only the film exists.

Perhaps for a moment you are pulled back "outside" the film, for example if a latecomer walks down your row to get a seat, or someone whispers too loudly near you. But soon the film reabsorbs you, and you and the film are again one. It is the job of the director and actors to ensure that you don't experience them acting. You have to buy into the illusion that they are actually the characters they are playing, so that they can receive 100 percent of your attention.

It is the same with our committee. If you pay attention, you can notice that there is this group of voices in your head. They are located "over there" somewhere, and you are "here" in a different place. (If people look carefully "where" the committee and they themselves reside, they will usually point out different locales inside or near the head. Curious, eh?) It is not that difficult to observe the voices (for a short time), but we have gotten so used to listening unconsciously to this internal "radio" program that we easily become fully reabsorbed in that ongoing internal conversation.

This full absorption is considered normal living. We will have to graduate from this semiconscious state if we want to evolve spiritually, however. Spiritual awakening involves a seemingly simple but deeply profound transformation in identity. That transformation begins with a change of perspective. In conventional living, we believe ourselves to be those speaking voices. Through spiritual practice, we come to discover that who we really are is the *listener* of those voices. When we understand that we are the listener, this change in perspective opens up a vast space heretofore not available in which we can come to know ourselves.

Listening to Your Committee

We all know how to listen. Sometimes, as in the movie example, we become absorbed in what we are listening to. At other times, we listen but maintain our separate stance from the speaker. We all have examples of being in a restaurant or coffee shop, on a bus or plane, and listening to a conversation happening near us. No big deal with that. I'm over here and there is a conversation, interesting or not, happening over there. That is the perspective you need to have regarding the conversation inside your head. Pretend it is happening at a nearby table.

Once you are able to separate the listening from the speaking and can experience those voices as separate from you as listener, you will soon discover certain things about that motley crew. As I've already said, they are not your most-evolved and intelligent friends, and you'll see that they never shut up. They have opinions about everyone and everything, most of all about you, and they are easily carried away by emotions. Also, they have absolutely no interest in facts or logic. Sound familiar?

It would be hilarious if it wasn't so tragic. You must be willing to face the embarrassment and humiliation that this group of voices is the management committee that has been running your life up to now, with your complicity and acquiescence. Please have the courage to take time to listen to those voices and discover that you are separate from them. Like an alcoholic who sets down the bottle for the last time, your hunger for authentic living will be strong enough to wean you away from the easy intoxication provided by the hypnosis of absorption in the committee.

As my students listen to their committee, they find that the members have distinct personalities, and some students will even give them names. They also can see that the members sometimes represent them at different times in their lives. At times, it may be the shy five-year-old talking; at other times, it is the rebellious teenager. In all cases, though, the members are smaller and lesser aspects of yourself.

Richard Axial

How to Escape Domination by the Committee

Most people will say they want to be "free," meaning free from domination, oppression, and undue influence. When they say this, they are thinking of outside forces trying to influence their actions. But, really, we have been completely dominated throughout our lives by this internal squad. The fact that the oppressor lives inside of us, rather than outside, does not alter the reality of our domination. The committee rules you. The "dog" is walking the owner.

True spiritual work begins with separating your consciousness from the noisy committee and strengthening your ability to stand separate. Most spiritual paths accomplish this through meditation. You just sit in a quiet place, free from distractions, and watch the committee do its thing. Every moment that you are watching it, you are not "in" it and so are strengthening your identity separate from the committee. For most people, this is a gradual process that takes place over some years. Sometimes you are able to watch it; other times you are pulled back in. You just have to persist in the exercise. Teachers call this observational stance vis-à-vis the committee by various names—watching, observing, noting—but the most common term is "witnessing."

Most of the women I teach have very busy lives. They are householders, active citizens and career people, not ashram devotees or monks, and they have no opportunity to spend hours in meditation or take long meditation retreats. So I work with them to develop their ability to witness the committee in real time. Throughout the day, whatever activity we are engaged in, whether alone or with others, the goal is to always have part of our awareness witness what the committee is saying, and never allow ourselves to be fully absorbed in the discussion. As we "witness" ourselves in this way, we also begin to notice other things, such as how we react when certain things are said, how easily an emotion can arise and subside, how reactions can make our bodies feel. As we continue to practice, we are examining our operating system in action and learning about ourselves. We can now see ourselves "from the outside" and are no longer limited to experiencing our life without conscious reflection. Over time, this witnessing process begins to assume a bigger and bigger presence in our lives.

Conscious Life

When you are able to observe your committee consistently over some length of time, you will discover that very little of value ever comes from that group. It has no usefulness whatsoever. It just endlessly ruminates, discusses, and opinionates. Yes, from time to time the group can stumble on to the "right" solution to an issue you are dealing with, but even in those instances, if you look closely at your process, you will find that you knew the right answer all along and truly did not need the committee's input.

You will also discover that there is a place of knowing within you that is separate from the committee's ruminations. It can show up as an instinctual knowing, or an answer can suddenly appear with no build-up or thinking process whatsoever. It just appears, and your whole body can feel its rightness. As we gain trust in our ability to know outside of the committee, we can discover that throughout our lives we had this capacity to know. But we didn't trust it, because the committee didn't validate it or because we were too distracted by the committee conversation to notice that we had access to better ways of knowing.

Seeker Story

I have been living "in my mind" most of my life. By this, I mean I was moving through the world with my mind as the operational headquarters and control room, from which spewed consistently negative ideas based on self-loathing judgments and opinions about mistakes, grudges, and anger from past events and fear/worry about future events. All of which I listened to and believed. I was rarely, if ever "in the now" unless I was forced to be in my demanding work as a photojournalist meeting deadlines for several large newspapers. I felt alone, imprisoned, depressed, scared, and battered by internal self-abuse, even though I wasn't consciously aware that I was living in this state.

Recently, at the end of a three-day retreat with this group, I had a meditation experience in which a very insistent communication came through as "Attention Must Be Paid." It sounded like a command from another dimension. I "heard" it say (though it wasn't words but more of a sense) that "they've been trying to reach me for so long, but I just haven't been paying attention." It felt as if a hole had been punched through the well-fortified brick wall of my internal mind prison. When I came out of my meditation and began to journal, I opened to a fresh page and saw a handwritten quote by author Arthur Miller that I had put in the journal about a decade ago. It read "Attention Must Be Paid." I cried and cried tears of grief for taking so long. And also tears of gratitude for the experience of seeing my own role in taking full responsibility for my life, well-being, and existence here.

Now, a few weeks later, I'm feeling as strong as 10,000 women. I'm able to breathe my teacher into my being during meditation (something I've never been able to do because I did not understand how). I feel as if I've stepped into a jet stream, and I'm being carried by life. I'm crying with strangers and feeling the deep, tender fierce love of all existence, love that understands that beauty and pain, truth and illusion reside next

> to each other all the time. It's as if I can now see and experience life as a beautiful, multilayered jewel that can look dull and black, but needs only to be turned a fraction of an inch to see an entirely new, sparkling, and radiant dimension.
>
> My body is responding to this new way of being with anxiety and shortness of breath. But with the guidance of my inner knowing and the deep love of my teacher and Spirit that so want my true self to emerge, I am trusting that my journey ahead is much more illuminated and radiant than the darkness of my own illusion from which I am emerging. Essentially, I feel liberated from the shackles of my own mind, from the illusion of my own dark mental prison. Even if the path ahead is not entirely bright, I know and trust my ability to handle whatever comes my way, because I am truly waking up. And I now know my true operational headquarters is in my heart.

You Are the Witness

As you continue and get more proficient with this witnessing, something remarkable happens. Initially, the witnessing feels like an intentional process that you "do." It is an active verb. You are "doing" witnessing, directing your attention to the committee. After a while, that activity begins to feel more like a presence. There is not merely an activity happening, but some *thing* is there as well. Behind the action of witnessing there is a deep, still, silent presence, a consciousness at work, an awareness, a being. As you continue to feel that presence, at some point along the way, you recognize that this presence or consciousness or being is *you*. You *are* the silent space that is present all the time, the one that listens and takes in but does not react. While the rest of your identity may fluctuate in all sorts of moods and feelings, this inner space is imperturbable.

By the time you have made this realization, you no doubt will have discovered what an essential aid witnessing is to the quality of your life. Once you have developed this capacity, at any instant you are able to either abide as the witness or be fully absorbed in what you are doing in that moment—driving, cooking, making love. In fact, when you are established as the witness you have more freedom to focus all of your attention on the activity of the moment. You can now let the dancer become the dance because you do not lose yourself when you are that dance. One moment you are the dance, the next second the witness. It all rests on where your attention is in that moment, because both the dancer and the witness occur simultaneously. You don't cease to exist when you dance or talk or cook, and you can drop into your witness at any moment without diminishment of the activity.

So now you can conduct your life while simultaneously witnessing it. Bravo for you! You have accomplished what few humans have.

Let us move on to the next step of our inquiry. Someone is witnessing, but who is that someone and what is her nature? As you continue to explore this feeling, you discover that this space (of you) is vast and deep. Indeed it is limitless. When you allow yourself to abide in that space and not be distracted by the committee, you can also feel its timelessness. In fact, it is timeless. It has always existed; it is a place outside of time. And it is you.

Seeker Story

Through the experience of learning to witness my own mind, I have come to understand that my mind is constantly on, observing a wide variety of things, commenting, judging, with a running commentary that could be likened to a broadcaster on a cable television station. Very early in my life, I had experiences of another aspect of myself, a compassionate Being, who watched from a quieter, deeper place without commenting. This deeper aspect had once guided me, but somehow, in the presence of an overly-active mental dialogue and an upbringing in a psychologically and emotionally abusive environment, I had lost touch with this inner aspect of who I am.

Learning to witness has been like learning to use a muscle I never knew I had. My mind would chatter incessantly, sometimes with relevant information (but most often not), and I would respond to the mental commentary as if it was me. I exercise this new muscle by regularly observing my mental chatter, while also knowing that the thoughts are not actually the true me.

The process of distancing my personal identity from what my mind has to say has opened up a great deal of inner space. I no longer feel enslaved by my mind. Instead, I see it is simply blathering to its own rhythm. It is doing its own thing. This has created space in my consciousness and my body for the true, deeper, more soulful part of me to emerge and guide my life. This is the self that was patiently watching things without comment for about four decades. It is the part of me that has been waiting for me to stop listening to my mind so that I could remember the true me and let that part of me BE the center from which I move through life.

In essence, I have shifted my mental awareness from an internal broadcasting station that spewed negative, trivial, and judgmental programming, to another, more soulful, attuned, and blissful source that connects me more closely with Spirit and my own divinity. Witnessing has helped me move from being a victim of my own programming and upbringing to the knowledge that I can tune the channel to whatever program best serves my spirit, family, and, ultimately, the world.

Side Note

Before we continue with this topic, I want to make an important point. In psychology, the goal is to have a coherent identity that functions effectively in the world. For people in conventional consciousness, this means their committee functions as one integrated identity. In other words, the person's identity is not fragmented. The individual knows there is a "me" and the various voices of the committee don't throw them into other, split-off identities. No matter what is happening with the inner voices, you know you are you. That is considered psychological health. It signals a well-functioning ego. Indeed, for people who are not able to achieve this developmental milestone, life can be challenging. Construction of that integrated identity is essential for healthy living.

But spiritual awakening takes us in another direction. The state of "health" that satisfies the need for psychological identity is not enough for the spiritually hungry. They sense and yearn for something more. Psychology requires that we construct a healthy ego. But spiritual training involves deconstructing that ego. So we have a bit of a paradox here. In order to become ego-less, we first have to have a robust, sound ego.

One of the problems spiritual teachers face is that some of their students have not accomplished the prerequisite of developing a mature healthy, integrated ego. In these cases, when the diminishment of the ego takes place through spiritual practice, the person's identity can weaken prematurely, before they can be established in their new identity as the witnessing presence, and a psychological breakdown can occur. Unfortunately, it is sometimes the case that the most psychologically fragile are the people most strongly drawn to spiritual work. Please be sure that you are truly ready for spiritual work. I often require that my students also have a therapist so that aspect of their lives will be well-tended.

With that caution, I want to return to the beginning of this chapter. In accomplishing this transformation in identity, you have not done away with the ego altogether. You have merely put it in its proper place as one tool that you use for functioning as a physical creature in this life. Think of it as your "advisory committee," which you can listen to or not. You are the boss, the one in charge of your life. This is quite a contrast to the previous situation in which you were lost inside of that group running you. In making this dramatic transformation in identity, you have begun to glimpse the Divine Essence within, a silent presence and awareness that feels familiar and deep. The awakening movement has begun.

Practice Suggestion

Witnessing is fundamental to spiritual advancement. Given that we are in the habit of being unconscious or unaware of what our committee mind is saying, it can be challenging to continue the witnessing practice for hours on end. One way to recover our witness is by making a conscious "reset" to the witness. The reset practice works like this: Whenever you end an activity or before you begin a new activity, pause for a moment to reset to your quiet center and reestablish your witness awareness. Before you pick up the phone, reset to center, and after the call, before moving on to the next thing, reset your consciousness to the still witness. Before you put your keys in the car ignition, reset, and do it again when you complete your journey. When you finish one task, doing dishes or writing a memo, reset before moving on to the next thing.

This resetting has a side benefit in that it interrupts moods that you could otherwise carry on indefinitely in an unconscious way. Returning to your center can be a valuable life practice as well as a spiritual tool.

10

GPS: Your New Compass for Living

As is true of any creature, our actions are intended to further our well-being and satisfy our needs of the moment. Though there will occasionally be times when we are completely satisfied and without further desires, that condition is not the norm and usually passes quickly. Most of our waking hours are spent in a never-ending quest to satisfy one desire/need/want/craving after another. As soon as one desire is satisfied, little time is spent in that satisfaction before another desire pops up, then another.

Most animals can be satisfied for a time. Their hunger can be satiated, their need for rest achieved. We humans are different because the root of most of our desires is not physical but psychological and conceptual. We can fill our stomachs and in so doing satiate the body's needs for sustenance, but the hungers of the mind cannot be so easily satisfied. Our capacity to imagine far exceeds our ability to fulfill those imaginings. A person can have a perfectly suitable home, but she can imagine (and long for) an even greater abode. A woman can have a wonderful mate, but will that stop her from yearning for an even better mate? And we know there is no closet that doesn't have room for another gorgeous outfit.

At the opposite end of the spectrum of our desires lie our dislikes. We don't want to be too cold or too hot; we don't want to be embarrassed; we don't want to drive an unreliable car or have to wear shabby clothes. <u>If our ego is not having us chasing after our desires, it is probably having us avoid what we don't like.</u>

Living this way is completely normal. As infants, our entire attention is focused on ourselves, on our wants and needs. As we mature, our focus expands to include some responsibility for others (share your toys…). Our main attention continues to be egocentric, however. So by "normal," I mean that this is how most people spend their lives, but not normal in the sense of healthy, fulfilling, or successful. Actually, the norm is an insane way to live. Yet we all do it.

A small child sees a rainbow in the sky and wants to "get there" and catch the rainbow. At some point in our young lives, we understand that the rainbow is an illusion of light that will always be beyond our grasp. As we approach, it recedes. Similarly, our desires are rainbows in our mind. We are always seeking the pot of gold that is just beyond our grasp. Even if we are able to grasp an object, for instance, buying a dress we want, the grasped object loses its magic allure, for it is desire itself we are trying to catch, not the object, and desire cannot be grasped. Like a ghostly spirit, it is too ephemeral. We reach out our hand, but the hand passes right through the ghost of desire.

HAPPINESS

Humans chart their actions with a compass, but one that is different from a magnetic compass. Our compass points to one direction called "I want," and whatever you most want in that moment is where the compass needle will point. (Remember the compass in *Pirates of the Caribbean*?) A desire pops into your head—for a latte, for a conversation with a friend, for your slippers, for a new bedspread—and your compass of desire will point you there, so off you go until the next desire pops up, and so then you head off in that new direction, and so forth, endlessly.

We humans laugh at a dog chasing its tail or a kitten a laser dot, but, truly, we are the more ridiculous. At least the dog has one constant desire: the tip of the tail. We are dogs chasing a multitude of ghostly tails that pop up and disappear without end. Yes, this is "normal" living for us.

Anyone who is spiritually advanced knows the folly of living thusly. They know that it is an exhausting and unsatisfying way to live, so they have graduated from this system and found another way to live. So I'd like to ask you: How do you like living this way, as a slave to ephemeral desires? Has it made you happy? Are you fulfilled and satisfied? How much of your day is spent trying to fulfill one desire after another or working so you can afford the things you desire (but don't truly need)? Do you want to spend the remainder of your life continuing this chase?

Of course, your ego committee tells you that you need these desires to be fulfilled before you can be happy. But do you? Are there really more conditions that must be put in place before you can allow yourself to experience happiness right now?

I imagine you have sometimes questioned this way of living, the endless pursuit of the ever-changing conditions of happiness. Many of us are caught up in the mob mentality in which everyone else is also madly pursuing their desires. When our interest flags, the momentum of the mob carries us along. If everyone else is chasing desire, then that must be the right thing to do. The humorist James Thurber wrote a short story, "The Day the Dam Broke." Someone, for whatever reason, starts running and yelling, "The dam broke." Soon the entire town is running in panic. The joke, of course (spoiler alert...) is that the town has no dam. This is what we and our friends and neighbors are doing, running away from our imagined dislikes as fast as we can and chasing our imagined desires. We, like the characters in the story, live in a society that has gone insane in its quest to satisfy more and more desires.

Give, Provide, Serve

For the sake of our own well-being and happiness, as well as the well-being of the planet, we have to find a new motivating force, a new ethos to guide our actions. I say we need to stop using that strange, erratic compass ("I want") and instead find a different instrument to guide us through life. In the same way that Global Positioning System (GPS) instruments have replaced the magnetic compass as our "go-to" devices to find our way about town and country, I have an instrument to propose to you, the initials of which are also GPS.

What I propose is the practice of "Give, Provide, Serve," or GPS. Let me explain. In any moment in time, you know what your "I want" system is urging you to do. For example, if you are in a conversation and one person says such and such, your mind will formulate what it wants to say in response. You may not actually say it, but it is in your mind. You may be at lunch with a group of friends and friend A says, "I think Mary _____" (fill in the blank with whatever content). Your mind will know what it wants to say about that topic. Let's imagine you stay quiet. Then friend B says "Oh, well, did you know Mary _____"" (again, what is said doesn't really matter). Now after this second comment your mind will again have a response, maybe the same, maybe different. But here's the important part: You will now feel more pressure from inside to share your remarks. And the longer the conversation is about Mary, the more irresistible it will feel to share your comments about her. There will be no discernment about whether you actually have anything useful to say, you will just have to talk in order to relieve the building desire to respond.

Whatever you say will come from your "I want" generator. Let's now look at a very different way to proceed. Imagine any scene where a conversation is going on among a small group of people. It could be a lunch with friends, as in the previous scene, or a meeting at work or a family dinner. It doesn't matter; just imagine something. Maybe you can remember a recent gathering.

Here's the discernment I would like you to have: At each moment in that conversation, pay attention to what your "I want" system would like to say. At the same moment, you also know what you could say (or not say) that would serve the entire conversation. That comment will likely be different from your "I want" perspective. Let's again pick up on our conversation about

Mary to illustrate this discernment. Suppose the group is commenting on a negative rumor about Mary, and the others have jumped in on the gossip. You too, from "I want" would like to add your juicy tidbit about Mary. Your higher intelligence knows, however, that Mary is a friend of the group and, whether the rumor is true or false, continuing this conversation will almost certainly cause harm to Mary. Instead of adding your salacious gossip about Mary, you make a positive comment about her that brings the topic to a close, and the group moves on to other subjects.

In acting this way you have practiced GPS. Here's how it works: In any situation, you look to see what is needed in that moment to further a positive result and assess whether you should be the one to provide it. Your perspective is "What does the situation need?" not "What do I want?"

For example, let's say you are in the supermarket checkout line and when you come to the cashier, you can tell that he is feeling worn out and bedraggled. You, too, have had a tiring day and you would prefer (I want) to slip through checkout as quickly and as invisibly as possible. Nevertheless, you practice GPS and have a brief, kind exchange with the clerk, which gives him a renewed sense of energy. You find that you, too, have elevated your own mood by this act of kindness. That's practicing GPS.

Another example: You are driving down the freeway in a foul mood (we've all been there, right?) and someone is frantically trying to cut in front of you so they can make the next exit. From your "I want" desire, you could cut them off and yell something rude about their inattentive driving. That might satisfy your immediate desire, but, in acting this way, you will add to the unhappiness and tension of the situation and to your own tension level. This is the price to be paid for feeling in the

[Handwritten at top: GPS — what is needed — next best action for all — includes self. ⭐]

WOMAN, GODDESS & SAVIOR

right. If you instead look to see what the situation needs, you will know that the right response is to get your frustration under control and allow the other driver to make the needed lane change.

In these two examples, I have shown that the kinder action is what was called for when practicing GPS, but that won't always be the case. Imagine a situation where you need to intervene forcefully but are afraid to do so. The "I want" response is to keep your mouth shut and avoid a confrontation, but, from your GPS perspective, you know you have to stand firm against some injustice. So GPS does not require a fixed type of response. Rather, it calls for a new perspective in living.

> **Seeker Story**
> GPS is more than just direction. "Give, Provide, Serve" has helped me navigate the world. When the question appears, "What should I do?" GPS can provide the answer. How can I provide what is needed in this situation? What can I do to be of service? What do I need to give (or give up)?
>
> This is different from the church teachings I learned as a child that stemmed mostly from fear and guilt. Be a good girl, don't make waves, and don't be selfish. That felt more like punishment. This feels more discerning. Maybe being stern with a child or telling the hard truth to a friend is the best way to provide. Maybe giving your time is more important than money. Maybe taking care of yourself will give you the energy you need to take care of others. When I listen for the answers to the question of what is most needed in this moment under the framework of Give, Provide, Serve, unexpected answers are revealed.

In ordinary life, people are relentlessly driven by what the committee of voices in their head insists is something they want or don't want. We simply yield to those thoughts and spend a lifetime being thrown this way and that, complaining that our desires are not being fulfilled and that our life is not all it should be. Of course, we can escape this madness for a time by sitting in disciplined meditation, but sooner or later we will have to get up from the mat and reengage with life, there to confront once again the committee that always craves more. Practicing GPS offers us another foundation for living, an alternative to our incessant egoic desires. Instead of acquiescing to these desires and complaints, we surrender to what conduct is needed from us to further the beneficial outcome of any situation. We practice GPS.

Living as Responsibility

Living as responsibility means taking responsibility for the situation you are in and what that situation calls for. This is a radically different perspective from acting on what you want for yourself. Humans are not isolated creatures. We live embedded in a network of relationships, and most of us live elbow to elbow with others in congested urban environments. In almost every waking moment, we are exchanging energies and mood vibrations with others. Living as responsibility means that you are sensitive to the people and environment around you and can sense what is needed in any situation. This is more of a feeling process than a thinking process. Intuitively, you will know what is needed. The only thing that blinds this intuition is the noisy volume of desire arising from your "I want" generator, as voiced by the committee.

Living responsibly is what any team spirit is about, the sacrifice of what each individual member wants in exchange for the success of the team. Most of us can act this way when we want to participate on a team. But we are on many teams for which we don't take responsibility. For example: the rush-hour commute team, the get-through-the-grocery-store team, the line-for-tickets team, or the share-space-at-the-buffet-table team. In these situations, can you also express the spirit of having the whole team win?

> **Seeker Story**
> I had one of those beautiful "thank god I'm open enough to connect when needed" moments at the airport this morning. A mother of two young boys was really struggling as one of them (about five years old) had an absolute meltdown on the airport floor. I watched her try to contain him while the other brother (six or seven) flapped about and looked distressed.
>
> After about five minutes of watching her trying to deal with this situation, I decided to see if she needed help. I bought her a bottle of water and went over. She was near tears and so grateful. I gave the distressed little guy my unopened yoghurt; sat with them for a few minutes and chatted calmly (the little guy stopped screaming at this point). After a while, I left my suitcase with her, and walked down the corridor with the older boy in search of an airport play structure. We found one, played for a bit, got him some water and a snack, plus a trip to the bathroom. About 15 minutes later I returned him safely to a calm environment. The mother just looked at me with tears in her eyes and said "thank you."
>
> I am soooo grateful to have the openness and presence to show up like this when it is needed.

The GPS Bet

When students come to me and it is time to begin the GPS practice, I ask them to conduct an experiment: the GPS bet. I ask them to try to practice GPS as much as possible and report back to me whether living in this way has given them more happiness than they achieved in the past by trying to fulfill their desires. So far, everyone has reported that their lives are more fulfilling, they are happier, they see how they make a difference to others, and they have a much fuller sense of contentment and connection. They feel freed from the prison of "I want."

This way of living is difficult, however, for the self-centered committee mind to grasp. It may be saying something like: "But won't this just make me a martyr? With everyone else acting selfishly and me acting for the good of all, won't I get used up?" Actually no, and here's why: You are part of the situation to which you are applying GPS and so your well-being has to be included as part of the solution. I'm not a fan of martyrdom, and I'm not asking you to always sacrifice your needs and well-being for the benefit of others. I'm just suggesting that you shift the focus from solely "me, me, me" to one in which you want everyone (including you) to win and experience some satisfaction. In GPS, we try to find the action that will result in the greatest amount of overall satisfaction.

For example, imagine a situation involving four participants. Outcome A will result in participant 1 having 100 satisfaction points, but participants 2, 3, and 4 having zero, giving a total of 100 satisfaction points, but three sour participants. Outcome B will result in participant 1 having 20 satisfaction points and participants 2, 3, and 4 each having 60 satisfaction points, for a total of 200 points. Isn't outcome B the better one? But what if you are participant 1, would you still support B? Obviously, this example is simplistic, but I hope it illustrates the point.

What would your family life be like if instead of every member selfishly trying to maximize his or her own desires, each of you was committed to the overall satisfaction of the family "team"? Instead of being competitors for satisfaction, the family members would truly be teammates for overall satisfaction.

> **Seeker Story**
> This practice has had a great impact on my life, particularly when it comes to making peace with decision-making. Having a selfless, service-oriented approach to how I get through my life really eliminates a great deal of the hemming and hawing and second-guessing that I often experience around planning and decision-making. It also allows me to truly show up for the people in my life. It regularly poses the question, "What serves this moment?" rather than "What do I want?" There is a tremendous sense of gratification and peace that comes with this orientation.

The Spiritual Importance of GPS

In the unawakened condition, people feel separate and isolated inside their own minds and bodies, cut off from the rest of existence. That is a very lonely and scary place to be, and their selfish actions arise from that delusion of separation. By contrast, in the awakened state, we see ourselves as a unity of existence, as a node in an omni-connected universe. In this state, we are never alone or separate. In this state, I know you to be me. If you and I are one, how could I choose actions that would make me happy but make you miserable? How can I be happy if you are not? If one child somewhere is hungry and frightened, how can I be completely satisfied? As an Awakened Being, I cannot. In the awakened state, the motto of the three musketeers applies: "One for all and all for one!"

This was the perspective of the great spiritual masters from past centuries who came up with their various versions of the Golden Rule: "Do unto others as you would have them do unto you." They were not preaching an injunction of sacrifice; rather an understanding of the true nature of happiness.

By practicing GPS, we not only find ourselves immediately more fulfilled and satisfied, we also are weaning ourselves from the delusion of separation and the habit of egoic self-centeredness. As we learn to feel more deeply into the needs of others, our love and compassion for them will naturally expand, and our heart will open.

GPS is a practice that you can do throughout the day, every day, and you will be given instant feedback from your surroundings about how well you are doing with it. GPS is the compass that points toward your awakening. Take the GPS bet. Just try it.

Practice Suggestions

Here are two suggestions to help you establish GPS as an ongoing practice:

1. As soon as you wake up, before you get out of bed, establish your intention to practice GPS. Maybe there are activities planned for the day. If so, run over in your mind how GPS might be applied to them. This should take only a few minutes.
2. Keep a daily journal of your GPS attempts. Practicing GPS can be a subtle activity, so recording your impressions, experiences, and feelings can be a helpful reference. Note when you tried it, how GPS differed from what you selfishly could have done, what impact you feel you had, and how you felt about yourself from the attempt. Do this for a month and review your notes to remind yourself of what progress you've made. You might be surprised.

11

Beauty Is Divinely Deep

There is a feminine beauty that is skin-deep, shallow, often artificially enhanced, and very perishable. But there is another kind of beauty that comes from deep within. It is the Divine Spirit emanating from you. This radiance is a gift to life that I ask my students to accept and express as a sacred offering to life. If you will permit this outshining, you will be beautiful, no matter your physical attributes or age.

Women awaken differently than do men. Elsewhere, we've discussed some of the reasons. The feminine qualities of service, surrender, cooperation, and openheartedness are the very qualities to be cultivated on the path to awakening. Also, women are somewhat freer of many of the qualities that plague men, such as chronic mistrust, competitiveness, and aggression. The loving heart of a woman is also closer to the heart of God than are the hearts of men.

Women have another significant advantage over men in the quest for awakening: their bodies. Women's bodies carry the energy of life, their bodies are manifestations of that life force, and they transmit that energy to those around them. This life force is the creative impulse of Universal Spirit. They are one and the same, differing only in degree. In this way, woman is always in resonance with God, and this harmonic is felt in her body.

Men's bodies are built for a different purpose than the life-giving, life-affirming body of a woman. Hence, men lack this natural connection with God. Nature keeps a woman from getting too disconnected from her body, whereas men can live more fully in their heads and can become quite removed from bodily feelings. If a man and a woman begin their spiritual work from an absolute beginner's place, the man starts at zero, but the woman begins her work already halfway to awakening. Her advantage is that great.

When a woman is genuinely happy or delighted (in good spirits), we can actually see and sense that glow of the Divine emanating from her, and her outshining brightens everyone present. Naturally and without effort, she radiates both the love and energy of God. She is a natural fountain of Divine Light and needs only to be feeling positive to have that fountain turned on. We have all experienced being in the delightful presence of such feminine light.

Seeker Story

When I began the beauty practice, I consciously did so in service of the Divine Feminine/Goddess. When I first started it, I noticed that heads literally turned in my direction—not only men, but also women and even children. When I dressed nicely, I noticed I felt better about my appearance. And when I felt better, I was more open to seeing others and being seen by them. I started practicing in the grocery store, in lines at the post office, walking in and out of gas stations, by simply seeing someone with openness (an open heart) instead of averting my eyes. When my gaze and presence was met, it became an open energetic greeting that felt so simple,

> sweet and real. It started to feel like I was being fed energetically by the exchange and that the other person was as well. It grew into a feeling of being able to move through the world with my inner light on, simply shining it outward in all directions.
>
> One day, while I sat in my therapist's waiting room, a little baby facing me in a car seat caught my eye. I started acknowledging the being inside this baby by *seeing* it and sending a sweet loving greeting to it. The baby started smiling and flirting and wouldn't take its eyes off of me. The baby's mother, who appeared to be in the therapist's office to address a sadness so significant that I could see it on her face, turned to me with a little smile and said, "She's never done that before with anyone," then she left for her appointment.

Women's bodies are beautiful to men and women alike. When animated with Spirit, women's bodies of all sizes, shapes, shades, and age are beautiful. However, fickle cultural standards of attractiveness, male crudity, and female competitiveness all conspire to make women hide their bodies, disguise their natural beauty with artificial appearances, and shut down their natural radiance. Almost all women are self-conscious about their bodies and tend to either hide or embellish their appearance, depending on the degree of confidence they have in that aspect of themselves. Either way, their natural radiance is suppressed. More's the pity about that, because the diminishment of the radiance of the feminine light results in all of us living in a dimmer world.

> **Seeker Story**
>
> A year or so into my time on this path I asked for a teaching on vanity. I was grappling with the subject, trying to find some spiritual orientation to a very sticky feminine issue. What I was expecting was the stock "spiritual" response of renunciation—detachment, a directive to shave my head and give my clothes away—something along those lines. What I got instead was a heart- and mind-opening revelation! The Beauty Practice: Do whatever it takes to truly feel like a goddess, and shine that beauty on the world as a healing offering. Then do it every day. Tears flowed down my cheeks, a smile beamed from my soul to my cheeks and beyond. It felt like a secret truth. And my relationship to primping and dressing changed drastically. Instead of egoistically judging myself in this process, I have learned to prepare for each day from a place of devotion, and as a prayer for the healing of the collective female wounds about body image and beauty. Such a gift of a teaching!

Beauty as Spiritual Practice

Since a woman's body confers such an important advantage for awakening, on the path that I teach we immediately take steps to turn that light back on. Living in a constricted, shutdown way serves no one—not the woman, not those around her. The women under my tutelage are supported to "let the Goddess come out and shine." First, they need to be encouraged to feel that energetic presence inside themselves, and once they can feel that presence, to let it radiate outward. I ask them to release their inner beauty and trust that its outer, physical expression is also beautiful, and then offer that beauty as their gift of light to life.

> **Seeker Story**
> The beauty project was a revelation to me. I always believed that caring about the way I appeared in the world was vain and superficial. It was something I struggled with until our teacher framed it in a different light. I came to understand that it wasn't about outer beauty, vanity, or trying to attract the opposite sex. It was about shining your inner light and making those around you feel good in your presence. Beauty is something everyone enjoys, whether it's a blossoming flower, a child's laughter, or a simple smile you share on a bus. The red lipstick only makes the smile within gleam brighter, and the flowing dress exposes the soft feminine within. I love the experience of smiling at a stranger and they contagiously smile back. For in that moment, we both feel better. Imagine if every moment was more beautiful just by shining your light.

Consistent with this offering, I ask them to have their physical appearance reflect that inner beauty. A movie star is always conscious of the effect they have on others when in public view, so they present themselves accordingly, and willingly offer the gift of their beauty. Similarly, my women students are asked to always look their best appropriate to the situation, whether in gardening clothes, teaching a school class, marketing, cooking dinner, or dancing at a formal ball. They are asked to remember that they are always making an impact on everyone around them, good or bad, all the time, so they must look their best as an ambassador of God.

Physical beauty, when it reflects a woman's Divine inner beauty and when offered free from ego or competitiveness, is a tremendous gift to life. The innocence of beauty, freely shared, touches every heart. With the right attitude adjustment and just a little bit of effort, every woman can give this gift every day. It is an act of Seva, or sacred service. Once a woman is willing to "let her Goddess shine," she will have made a great leap toward her enlightenment. Her confidence and feeling of mastery of life will grow.

It will take little extra effort on your part. So please be generous with your life force and your beauty. We all need that nourishment.

> **Seeker Story**
> Like many women, I have had a love-hate relationship with my body since I was a teenager. If my reflection in the mirror looks good on any given day, or I'm feeling adequately thin enough, or I've exercised for several days in a row, then I feel good. Conversely, feeling bloated, flabby, or with a closet full of clothes that don't fit is an immediate invitation for a grumpy-sad-withdrawn mood to set in. It's been a nearly daily yo-yo ride where I just kept thinking, "If only I was ____ enough, I would feel good." The idea that my feminine beauty can be an *offering* to the world is a complete flip of that obsessive me-focused view. Wearing clothes that make me feel beautiful or even sexy, smiling brightly into the world, and letting my heart shine, even extending it to creating beautiful spaces in my home and garden, is about bringing joy to *other people*. Mind you, I have decades of my own critical eye in the mirror to unravel, but I totally get that by consciously bringing my own expression of beauty into the world, and feeding our intrinsic human nature to appreciate that beauty...I am helping to create a more positive, loving world.

The feminine senses and creates beauty, and the wise woman sees this as one of her most important gifts to the world. When a woman freely radiates her natural beauty as a spiritual offering, her sense of beauty everywhere is heightened. She sees the beauty in others and in her surroundings, and she is nourished by that sensitivity. Where others can see only monochromatic dullness and ugliness, she sees the beauty in everyone and everything. She naturally adds beauty to her surroundings and in so doing makes both her personal radiance and her environment a welcoming experience for others. Through the beauty that she exudes, builds and beholds, her heart of love opens, and she will know the face of the Divine.

12

Sex and the Spiritual Girl

The issue of sex often comes up in spiritual groups, so let's delve into that topic for a moment. Over a half century ago, Helen Gurley Brown's wildly popular and provocative book *Sex and the Single Girl* challenged the cultural norms of its day. It advocated the naturalness of an active sexual life for adult single women, who society expected to live in a state of sexual celibacy until the "right" men came along and claimed them in marriage. Today, we can look back with a kind of superior bemusement at the unrealistic and quaint, repressive moral expectations that neo-Victorian, mid-century society imposed on single women.

In our time, the residue of those repressive expectations are still in place, especially in the religious and spiritual domains of life. Let's look at why this is so and how those attitudes can hinder women's spiritual development. As I noted before, men tend to favor more ascetic practices and diminishment of their engagement with life, and so tend to look with disfavor on sexual activity while on a spiritual path. We humans are among the animal kingdom's most sexually active species, however. We and our primate cousins, the bonobos (a species of chimpanzee), seem to be without equal in our avid pursuit of sexual pleasure. Until the last half-century and the advent of reliable birth control, lots of sex naturally resulted in lots of children, and children meant a lifetime full of resource-gathering and householder duties necessary to get those offspring to adulthood, leaving little time and energy for spiritual inquiry.

Religions throughout the ages have had to come to grips with this fact of life. The response by many was to separate religious seekers from everyday life and into a more cloistered existence where their time and energy could be reserved for spiritual growth, not raising children. This segregation also typically meant separation of the sexes in order to minimize the opportunity for romantic stirrings and sexual liaisons. Some religious groups also codified into their doctrines the requirement of total sexual abstinence by their acolytes—a prescribed life of celibacy.

It is easy to understand how our spiritual institutions came to see humans' robust sexual drive as an adversary. Even more, the body itself came to be seen as the enemy, as something evil and corrupt. The choice was bodily expression *or* god, not both.

Biologically speaking, our active sexuality was an evolutionary breakthrough for our species, rather than a perverse burden. Along with our big brains, opposable thumbs, and hips and heels made for walking, our "always on" sexuality was one of the "big four" evolutionary breakthroughs that made our species possible. Without this sexuality, the flourishing of our species arguably could not have happened.

Today we live in an era of reliable birth control, so unplanned pregnancies can be a thing of the past for responsible couples. That technology has opened up an unprecedented opportunity to use our natural, robust sexual impulse in service to our spiritual advancement, rather than regarding it as a hindrance. This is especially true for women who, as we have seen, tend to awaken more naturally through their bodies and hearts rather than through pure consciousness. In fact, our biological gender and impulse for domestic partnership can become valuable assets in the spiritual quest, rather than the hindrances they were believed to be in the past.

Partnering for Awakening

Sex can be used for procreation, pleasure, or illumination. Men and women form conventional relationships out of a combination of bodily instincts and egoic desires, and their relationships thrive or wither depending on the extent to which each partner's desires are fulfilled. These two fundamental energies underlying relationships could be described as "body meets body" and "ego meets ego." But there is another impulse that can bring men and women together: the Divine Impulse that abides in the innermost core of each of us. In the helter-skelter busyness of daily life, few people are conscious of that impulse, and fewer still will live by its call and awaken to their Divine Essence.

For those who are stirred by that call of Spirit, the typical man-woman relationship based on the limited energies of instinct and ego is unlikely to be fully satisfying. In fact, such relationships can be a hindrance to spiritual realization—so much so, that often the process of spiritual ascent is believed to be a solitary journey and one completely independent of gender.

One's gender and intimate relationships can in fact be used as energy to power the liberation of the Divine Impulse. As we each possess in ourselves a predominately feminine or masculine essence, one channel of flow for the energy of Spirit is through this gender aspect of our humanity. Of course, humans have other attributes through which Divine energy can flow, such as compassion, wisdom, and parental care, but those expressions are not the topic of this chapter. Rather, we are now focusing on one very specific and important aspect of humans: our gender polarity. The spiritual path that I teach is very sex-positive. We encourage women to fully embody their sexual nature and see it as a growing spiritual light. A woman becomes a Divine sexual being, the Goddess.

Sex as a Tool for Awakening

As we discussed in the chapter on beautiful service, your life energy, when shared from a place of love and compassion, is a gift, a blessing to all who come into its domain. This gift includes the sexual and sensual energy that you radiate. Sexual energy expressed from the ego and used competitively or to seduce is completely different from the sexual/sensual energy that flows from the Goddess as You. It is an enlivened offering from your depth of love. Just enjoy being that.

A woman's sexual nature and energy can also be a great source of power to awaken her to her Goddess nature, as well as intensify her connection with the Earth. However, this very powerful force must be used wisely. Sex is pleasurable and in it there exists the possibility of union with another person, so it can be a most fruitful arena for opening to ego transcendence and Divine Love. In earlier chapters, we talked about the feminine preference for awakening in the heart (Love) and body (Eros). Opening your heart in a feeling of love for a cherished partner and opening your heart to infusion by Universal Love are somewhat analogous experiences. Similarly, surrendering your body in ecstasy to a caring lover and surrendering your body to the Divine Impulse as Eros, the universal energy of creation, are also somewhat comparable experiences.

Seeker Story

I have always enjoyed sex and appreciate its many meaningful benefits. It's been my relational basis for comfort, connection, and security, as well as being delicious. And yet ordinary sex can also feel very similar to fast food: It may satisfy the hunger momentarily, but ultimately can leave you feeling undernourished. Sex for spiritual illumination opened me to a whole different world. The connection between body and spirit during conscious lovemaking takes the experience to a level beyond the self. In fact, it can sometimes feel as if there is no longer a "self." This kind of lovemaking is an opportunity to converge with the divine—the divine in each of us and also the divine entity created by our union.

Of all the important components needed to cultivate the fertile soil for enlightened sex, the love that already exists or is being created in that moment is surely the most valuable. For my partner and me, it is the foundation that allows for the experience to unfold. We have established the trust and safety that is so necessary for each of us to surrender fully and eventually dissolve into oneness. Slowing way down in movement and breath allows for the consciousness to emerge and the magic to happen. Also, it helps for us to let go of any agenda or the feeling of needing to reciprocate. Following our own desires so fully that we actually get lost in the experience allows the divine energy to flow between us. The moment transcends space and time, as if our bodies are no longer boundaries and time stands still in eternity. The "I" dissolves completely into the Oneness of all that is—and the feeling is something like waves of pleasure pushing beyond each edge that appears. Our bodies merge into a field of energy that lives beyond the confines of us as individuals. This is divine union of two souls and God thru the portal of sex.

It is easy to understand how human sexual union, when done with integrity, full consciousness, and in a context of spiritual growth, can be a valuable "practice field" so to speak, for opening to Divine Eros and Love. On the path that I teach, I encourage women to fully embrace their sexuality and utilize their committed romantic partnerships for sexual/sensual exploration leading to spiritual illumination (usually to the delight of their partners).

Sexual embrace with a loving and trusted partner can also be practiced by the woman in order to experiment with greater surrender of the body and to experience more profound "letting go" of the ego's controls over the body. As the woman learns to trust in the power of surrender, she can more fully open to the infusion of Divine Goddess Energy that desires to fill her. This Divine potential is what she has always longed for from her depth (and probably searched for in other domains without success), but which her ego has always feared.

In order to explore this sacred domain, she will benefit from a skillful lover who can be sensitive to this yes-no fluctuation and who can lovingly support her yearning for spiritual surrender, while also honoring her fear when it arises. In surrendering to a conscious lover, a woman opens the gates of separation to meet and transcend her fears, limitations, and mistrust.

When the energy of Spirit is welcomed into the body and heart, it can animate you in all of your expressions of the life force. When this first happens and until your body adjusts to this infusion, you may feel like a cat on catnip. Imagine the Goddess flowing through you in full arousal yelling, "Yahoo!"

Sometimes that catnip state can lead to an explosion of sexual energy. The Goddess can be one very lusty lady. If this happens to you, having an understanding partner, a wise teacher, and the holding by your dear spiritual sisters will be invaluable support during this transition time while your body adjusts to its higher vibration. Until your physicality and consciousness can accommodate this expansion of sexual energy, existing relationships and their agreements can sometimes be severely challenged.

Misuse of Sex

In addition to using sex for procreation, pleasure, or illumination, we humans have also misused sex in a multiplicity of ways. Each of us has only to look at our own sexual history to find examples. Discussing and examining the variety of such actions and their underlying motives, strategies, and mores would take an encyclopedia of commentary, so we will limit our inquiry on the topic to the misuse of sex in spiritual schools: the potential for an unhealthy sexual relationship to occur between students or between students and a teacher. As noted, humans are a sexually voracious species. Whenever masculine and feminine polarities come together, the current of sexual energies will arise. It is easy to get lost in a never-ending hedonistic pursuit of sexual pleasure. The wise seeker, however, will keep her eyes on the real prize of awakening, and have her sexual expression serve that end.

In addition, many human females have a natural attraction for "alpha males." Like our primate cousins, certain females of our species have always sought the good graces of the dominant male(s), and that sometimes includes sexual favors. Realistically, we have to accept the inevitable that society will never eliminate sexual relations between bosses and their assistants, between professors and students, between political leaders and their staff members, and between gurus and their devotees. Power has been an aphrodisiac since the dawn of our species.

In my view, the problem for spiritual communities stems from the issues of (1) general unease about sex and spirit, (2) hypocrisy, or (3) exploitation. Regarding the first, I have already covered that. While I understand the history behind the separation of sex from religion, I see sex as a valuable (though somewhat risky) tool for spiritual awakening.

Regarding hypocrisy, scarcely a month goes by without there being some news story about a minister, priest, or other religious authority figure who gets caught with his pants down. The aspect that makes these instances newsworthy is that the offender has not been practicing what he preaches. He may have taken a vow of celibacy or preached against extramarital relations, condemned same-sex liaisons, or advocated for abstinence. Most assuredly, he should be held accountable for his hypocritical violation of the code he advocates and professes to live by.

We also occasionally hear news stories about spiritual teachers who sexually exploit their devotees. Here also, most of these news stories concern teachers who have taken vows that prohibit such liaisons. However, there are also stories of teachers exploiting the trust and beliefs of their students in order to engage in sex. If you come across a teacher, man or woman, who tells you that the only way to awaken is to have sex with him or her, it is time to roll up your meditation mat and go elsewhere.

Though there is no doubt some sexual exploitation by spiritual teachers, it is also true (whether people want to hear this or not) that having a loving and responsible, consensual sexual relationship with a spiritual teacher can, under certain circumstances, have a beneficial effect on spiritual growth. We have to understand that a guru-devotee relationship is based on love, the deep love of soul to soul. The definition of guru is "one who brings illumination," and that can stir a student to her core. As with any relationship in which a man and woman work closely together for a noble cause, respect and love are bound to grow.

Of course, these factors do not have to lead to sex, and in practice they rarely do. But sexual attraction is sometimes bound to happen between a teacher and student. In these cases, both parties need to act in the highest integrity and with the consent of all individuals affected. The final burden of responsibility for the success of these encounters needs to lie with the teacher, even when the initiative comes from the student, as it often does. Sex is a powerful, powerful force in our lives, and most people have some degree of wounding in this area, so teachers must be at their wisest and in their highest integrity before engaging in consensual sexual intimacy with any students.

The path that I teach has definite tantric leanings, meaning that I encourage my students to utilize the inherent pleasurableness of sex, engaging in sacred practices with their committed partners to further their spiritual illumination and their awakening as Eros and Love.

That attitude is not suitable for everyone, however. Many, if not most, spiritual teachers will not agree with this approach. Also, some students will want the security and safety of a sex-free spiritual environment. Others may want some active engagement of their bodies in their spiritual practice, but activities such as yoga or ecstatic dance may be perfectly adequate forms for them. Therefore, when you are searching for the spiritual path that will best suit you, you will want to choose a group whose attitudes toward sexuality and awakening are compatible with yours. There is such a wide range of offerings in this regard that you are bound to find one to your liking. Since sex is such a powerful aspect of our human makeup, please take the time to inquire with prospective teachers what their stance is regarding sex and spirituality.

Tantra

Tantric spiritual paths have been around for several millennia. Tantric schools in Buddhism and Hinduism did not follow the customary path of renunciation in order to achieve enlightenment and instead embraced the full panoply of life's experiences, including bodily desires, sensations, emotions, and other expressions of humanness as tools for awakening. In these schools, the path could be rigorous indeed.

In many Western nations today, we are still emerging from centuries of puritanical repression of our sexual expression. No surprise, then, that when Westerners stumbled across the ancient tantric traditions and their acceptance of all of life's energies, they focused on one aspect of tantrism practiced in a minority of these schools: the embrace of sexual energies as a tool for awakening. In the veritable blink of an eye, many of these seekers, after having a brush of familiarity with tantric texts or teachers, proclaimed themselves to be enlightened teachers of "tantra," which now meant the teaching of advanced techniques of sexual pleasure, all wrapped up in the legitimizing robe of spirituality. In other words, you don't have to feel guilty about having pleasure in sex because it is "spiritual."

Commentators now tend to call such Western expressions of tantra "neo-tantra" (or pop tantra or California tantra). If you see workshops advertising tantra, chances are that it will be new-age neo-tantra you will be learning, not ancient traditional (and generally secret) teachings. When seekers come across these "tantric" courses and workshops they should expect them to be more in the nature of Kama Sutra workshops, not esoteric tantric spiritual teachings.

I have nothing against people becoming better lovers and incorporating sexual union as part of their spiritual practice. As I said, I encourage that in my teaching. Many people would benefit greatly from becoming more skilled and intimate lovers, so Kama Sutra workshops on sexual technique can be a good thing. I am disappointed, however, when the noble word *tantra* is used for these less-than-spiritual purposes. The true goal of traditional tantra is embodied spiritual awakening, not mere orgasmic ecstasy.

13

Diving into the Darkness

Spiritual awakening is typically viewed as a journey into the light, hence the words *en-lighten-ment, waking up, illumination,* and similar descriptions of a path upward to the light. The spiritual life is imagined to be a process of purification, leading to a condition of pure goodness and wisdom. The novice seeker may believe that spiritual practices will result in the shedding of the dense, "bad," and unwanted aspects of herself, leaving only desirable qualities. Due to this widespread misconception, spiritual aspirants are often surprised to learn that it is sometimes necessary to face their negative side, their dark "shadow."

In addition to unpleasant memories we may have of past traumatic experiences that we try to suppress or perhaps have even walled off completely, most of us have aspects of ourselves that we fear, loathe, mistrust, hate, or feel shame or embarrassment about. We may even feel like we have an evil twin inside that we have tried to keep bottled up or hidden throughout our life. Or we may be in total denial of those qualities, having banished them from our consciousness. Of course, these imaginings and judgments are products of our ego committee, and everyone's committee has many, many opinions about how we should and shouldn't be. As a result, there are aspects of ourselves that we suppress and deny. Our egos hope that spiritual efforts will enable those aspects to melt away magically, thus freeing ourselves of them forever.

Many of us do not want to face our negative characteristics. Indeed, this avoidance is sometimes a principal motive for entering spiritual work. We teachers call this desire to avoid one's messiness "spiritual bypass." I'm sorry to inform you that this is an unrealistic expectation. In both psychological therapy and in spiritual realization, many of us must journey through the dark and messy shadow aspects of ourselves that heretofore we sought to avoid at all costs.

> **Seeker Story**
> After a period of meditation, we were asked to write down our roadblocks to awakening—what's in the way of our spiritual journey. As soon as I started writing down my barriers, a broad smile came across my face. I suddenly knew that everything I began to write down—my need to be right, my ego, my individuality, my attachment to anything and everything, my fear of losing control/being controlled, of not mattering, of losing myself—are also all perfect resources for my spiritual journey. All of them contribute to the path by way of frustration, patience, blame, forgiveness, entitlement, gratitude, exhaustion, devotion, and awakening. My life—exactly as it is, the whole hot mess—is the perfect fertile ground for my own awakening. Everything and everyone is here in front of me as my teacher.

A spiritual practice, like therapy, opens up our consciousness. When we open, both good and bad qualities and memories may be revealed. Of course, the good memories are pleasant and are not an issue. The descent into the darkness of ourselves, however, can be painful, chaotic, and terrifying and give rise to hopelessness and despair. But—and here is the important point—this descent can also provide the moist, fertile ground in which our Divinity can take root and grow.

Some people may think of enlightenment as something that happens only after a person has endured decades (or lifetimes) of purification, during which time they shed all of the unwholesome aspects of themselves. The path that I teach goes about awakening in a different manner. We embrace the totality of ourselves, the good, the bad, and the ugly. This person—who you are in this moment—is the being who will awaken, not some idealized conception of a more perfect future you. The focus that is needed for this spiritual work is self-acceptance, rather than correction. As you open more and more to the inner Divine Presence, a natural, organic transformation will begin, a process not dictated by your ego, but one inspired by Grace. You and your "evil twin" will not have to live estranged and in perpetual conflict, but will be joined and transformed in a new birth as the Divinely-Awakened One.

> **Seeker Story**
> The longer I do this work of spiritual awakening, the more I realize that it is akin to birthing my true self from the womb of my existence while engaged in the fabric of everyday life. There are so many parallels to the birthing process I went through in bringing my own daughter into the world. I feel an inner longing deep within that wants to emerge. This is life force energy, and it feels like carrying a child. It is a sense of longing to meet the life force, of being energized and enlivened by it without even knowing what lies ahead.

> Four years into this work, I am seeing the pattern: I expand, I contract. When I expand, I feel amazing, connected to the magic web of life. The wind tickles my skin and I'm in love with the world in the way I was in love with my new baby. When I contract, I am living in my own personal hell. My mind goes wild with all sorts of thoughts and egoic voices. I feel immature and vulnerable, angry and incapable. I feel separate.
>
> Bringing a baby into the world has taught me that I am strong enough to continue this new kind of birthing journey, and I remain excited about the unknown possibilities. I try to go easy on myself even when in a week-long contraction. I try to practice the surrender I learned in birthing. On the back end of a contraction, I'm a little more open, a little wiser, a lot more psychic, and, ultimately, somewhat further down the path of ultimate surrender. I wonder if these contractions will end when I truly surrender. Perhaps this is where the birth of my true self lies.
>
> Seeing this pattern is helping me understand the larger flow of life and the endless possibilities that emerge out of the same dark void of nothingness and creation from which my daughter — and, in fact, all living beings — are born.

The process of spiritual awakening has much in common with the archetypal hero's journey of mythology. The hero departs from the safety of the community to face trials, tests, purifications, and initiations. Sometimes even death and resurrection must be experienced before the quest is fulfilled and the hero returns to the community reborn.

Such a journey requires courage, trust, persistence, and faith. The spiritual quest is no different in this regard. Spiritual awakening involves the metaphoric "death" of the personal self as well as rebirth as the Goddess. Like any pregnancy and birth, a lot of discomfort, pain, and messiness often accompany the "miracle of creation."

During your journey, your teacher will be your mentor, holding you in love while providing essential guidance. You will also have allies in your spiritual sisters, many of whom will have trod this path before you and who will be holding you with love and acceptance. And you will also be blessed with Divine Love, which will greet the worst of you with infinite compassion and love. As you reveal the shadow aspects of yourself and discover that you are still loved, valued, and honored by your spiritual companions, the negative self-judgments begin to soften and melt, and true wholeness emerges.

In addition to the encounter with the personal shadow, the journey for some seekers can also include occasional confrontations with the collective shadow forces that create pain and suffering in our communities, nations, and world. Again, have trust that these encounters are important for your spiritual growth, bear them, and utilize the support of your teacher and colleagues.

Every person is unique, so we cannot anticipate whether our ventures into the darkness will be many or few, intense or mild. Whatever the quality of our "night patrols," let us take heart in knowing that they almost always have a purpose and potential to further our spiritual growth. So do not let yourself become discouraged if your "journey into the light" becomes a "dark night of the soul" from time to time. Have trust in the wisdom and love of your teacher, and have faith that such experiences are simply grist for the mill of your awakening as the Goddess. They, too, shall pass.

14

The Story of You

To begin my life with the beginning of my life, I record that I was born... So says that master storyteller Charles Dickens in the first paragraph of *David Copperfield*.

Like Dickens, you also are a master storyteller. You have been actively creating your masterpiece of a tale, the epic and mythic fable of your life as it has unfolded. However, unlike Dickens, who knew his character was a fiction, you believe your main character is real. You believe she is real because she is you.

Dickens wrote his tale in book form, but today you can also buy it as an audio narrative. Your epic has not been published in printed form and exists only as an audio/video narrative that lives inside your head. Over time, bits and pieces of that autobiography may be shared with others, but the full narrative is stored and accessed in internal files retrievable only by you.

As a child you probably read series novels or watched long-running television series that followed a character through many books or episodes. Think of the Nancy Drew mysteries or *The Simpsons* television series. Each book or segment follows and further develops the character described in the earlier works. After a while, there is not much more of the character that can be developed, and the writer is challenged to keep the audience interested. So it is with us as well.

Beginning in early childhood, but proceeding in earnest around the time of middle school, we engage in a life-long negotiation with our environment about who we will come to be. We pit our desires against the feedback we receive from our family, friends, and teachers, combining that with our various life experiences to fabricate, invent really, a character that makes the most sense given all that diverse input and experience. We compare our internal feelings with the feedback from those around us, and we create a compromise identity that we can live with and those who know us can also accept. We give that character our name. From now on, we will act our lives as this composite character and stifle those aspects of ourselves that are not consistent with the role we are playing. In so doing, we "knit" ourselves to the world around us. Though we may have previously felt like a fish out of water, with the invention of our compromise character we now fit in; we belong. We know who we are and our place in the world. This is accomplished, however, at the cost of our authenticity.

The real you will now be hidden in the background, and people will see only the character you are performing. Over time, you will learn to "stay in character," forget the existence of your authentic self and come to believe that you actually are the character you created. It may seem impossible that you could forget yourself, but it is, sadly, all too common. Indeed, it is standard child-rearing practice to "mold" the child into what the family and community desire. Let's look in more detail to understand how you can become completely lost to yourself.

The Nature of Memory

Here's how your story grows: You have an experience, and your immediate memory of what happened may at first resemble how others present would also describe what happened — resemble, but not exactly match, so your description of the external event will be somewhat unique. In addition, you had internal responses to the external happening, and no one else will have that. This is the second tier of the story, your unique inner experience. Then you add a third tier to the experience: meaning. You place that experience in relationship to the story of your life and the beliefs you have about yourself and your environment, and you assign a value, meaning, and context to your experience.

Each significant experience of your life is thus recorded on three levels: the outside aspects of it, in which your experience will differ to some degree from others who may have been present; the inner experience, which is solely yours; and the meaning of it, which is a pure creation of your imagination. With every experience, the solidity of the character you have invented and given your name to deepens, as each new experience further defines that character.

Repeat this process several thousand times a year — year after year — and it becomes obvious that you will have created an internal representation of a lifetime. However, it is the fictional lifetime of a fictional character to whom you have given your name. That character lives nowhere else. It does not have existence outside of your imagination.

This brings us back to Dickens. He knew his character was fictional, but you no longer register any difference between your storyline character and yourself, and you believe your authored self to be real. As life proceeds, you live it as that character, not as your authentic self. Your attributes are the character's attributes, your experiences the character's experiences. In a very real and tragic sense, you have ceased to live a true life and instead have become the actor, playing the role of your character. In so doing, you have resigned yourself to acting out the life of the character you created. Meanwhile, your authentic self is locked in a cell deep within your inner fortress, while the false character lives the life that should rightfully be yours.

Inventing Your World

What you gain by this is that you know how to act. In other words, you know what your character would do in the novel of your life. You know what is expected of you. But that is not the end of it. While you have been creating your main character, you have also been fabricating the world in which she lives, the background scenery in which her saga plays out. It is not the real world in which you are living; it is a virtual world that is a product of your imagination. Of course, there has to be some basic correspondence between your imagined world and true reality. You cannot believe you can fly or walk on water. Reality quickly dashes such unrealistic conclusions. But the overlap between your inner reality and true reality can be surprisingly small. Despite that, our invented world receives enough validation and confirmation for us to be able to confidently assure ourselves that we are accurately interpreting reality. So we believe that the world in which we exist is the same world that exists for everyone else.

You also populate this world by creating stories about everyone else in your life—your family, friends, coworkers, and groups of people—lawyers, sales clerks, policemen, bus drivers. When you interact with anyone, you are not actually responding to who they are being in that moment. No, you are reacting to your invented story about them, and you are fitting whatever is happening in the present moment into the parameters of the characters you have invented for them.

Similarly, they are relating to you from their story about you, which won't exactly match up with your self-story. They are also relating to you from inside the imaginary world they inhabit, which can be a very different world than yours. The dissonance between the various stories invented by you and by others creates endless conflict and tension as all these stories compete for their version to be the "real" story, the true reality. The consequence of living in such a multi-storied world is that no one is actually acting on what is truly present in the moment. The stories trump the reality in front of us.

Almost everyone lives in such a representational, imaginary virtual world. Spiritual teachers talk about how we are all living in a dream world, and this is part of what they mean. Let's now look at how your ego constructs such a life.

The Hunger for Authentic Experience

The ego is a storehouse of memories of experiences. Everything you have ever experienced is stored there, ready for retrieval. The ego is also eager to save you the work of actually experiencing life, strange as that may sound, so it offers you a shortcut. Let's imagine for example that you are biting into a peach for the very first time. You feel the strange fuzziness of its skin and register its particular smell; the new flavor bursts into your mouth. As you bite in, you taste the unique combination of flavors—sharpness and sweetness; you feel the juice roll down your chin, and you note whether you like this new eating sensation. This process absorbs quite a lot of your attention. Meanwhile, your ego has recorded all of this.

Some weeks later you eat a second peach. The sensations are still happening, but this time there is something else going on. Your ego is comparing today's sensation with its stored record of the first peach and noting the differences, if any. Once you have eaten a small number of peaches, the ego now has all the data it feels it needs about peaches, so it does not even bother allocating attention to the experience at hand. Instead of feeling what is actually happening with a new peach in your mouth now, the ego just serves up its composite memory of a peach. The experience of your taste buds never travels past the ego. No sensing or experiencing is happening at all—only memories. Psychologists call this process "apperception." No new encounter is experienced "raw" so to speak; rather, it is integrated into the existing store of experience to form an updated, synthesized whole.

It is this way with everything in life. Novel encounters can still be authentically experienced because the ego is not familiar with them and has no memory stored. With everything else, however, the lazy ego simply regurgitates the memory of previous similar experiences and doesn't bother to register what is actually happening now. Whether it is input from the five senses or your emotional responses to life, it is actually stored memories you are "feeling," not the actual input from your nervous system.

Have you ever wondered why first-time experiences are so vivid and alive, but when experienced again seem duller and monochromatic? Whether it is your first roller coaster ride, first kiss, first oyster, or first snowman, the ones that follow don't seem to have the same vividness or intensity. Memories, like movie sequels, rarely live up to the original.

WOMAN, GODDESS & SAVIOR

As the years go by and you accumulate more experiences, it becomes rarer to have new and unique encounters with life. Instead, repetition is your daily fare. When you live mostly in the recalled past, your hunger grows for the authentic, for true living, for the experience of being alive. Every one of those compiled memories has the additional function of defining the character through whom you are living. You, as that character, know whether or not you like peaches, or walking on sand, or Woody Allen movies, or people from New York. Each of those conclusions boxes you in, further reducing the likelihood of your encountering a new experience. "I do/don't like _____ (fill in the blank)." After the first dozen books or so, how much latitude would the Nancy Drew author have to express new aspects of Nancy or give her new opinions? How much do you? Consistency and predictability trump reality.

Your true self wants to live, but she is hemmed in by the limits imposed on your character. You are sick of repetition, but feel trapped in it. Your hunger for authentic living and the feeling of being truly alive are what draw you to new adventures — to travel to new places, have an affair, buy something new, or take up a new hobby — because it is only with something new or novel that you can, at least for a moment, again authentically experience life.

Oftentimes these adventures are to your detriment, and they are not lasting. That new affair will soon no longer be new; the new dress will become the old dress at the back of the closet. Wouldn't it be better if you could experience *every moment* as if it were new? Wouldn't life be more engaging if you could be in the present moment, without that moment being diluted by the past? Such aliveness could be possible for you, but first we have to talk about how memories work.

Richard Axial

Memories Are Tricky Things

We tend to think of our memories as something solid and unchanging, like a photograph or video recording of an event. As noted, however, memories are a much more creative and dynamic process than being mere recordings. We all know that when many people witness an event, their impressions of the same event can vary widely. No one exactly captures the actual event, only her or his imperfect impression of it. In addition, even the witnessed accounts will change over time. Memories "drift"; they don't stay in place. Usually, we aren't conscious of that. When we recall memories of an event from last year, or 10 or 20 years ago, the current version of the memory of that event will not be the same as previous versions. Since we don't recall the earlier versions, we believe that what we are remembering today is what actually happened back then. This is the first error in the story of you. Your memories of both the externals of an event and your internal reactions were misperceived from the get-go and have further eroded from the actuality since that time.

Motives and self-interest also distort memories. We are self-serving in our version of events and tend to put the best face on our actions. That self-serving justification also evolves over time.

If you look at a memory, what you see is a story, a vignette. It can be long or short, but will usually be in the form of a story as experienced by you. When you are in the grip of a memory, you are to some degree reliving an incident from the past. If you spoke about it, it would come out in a story format. But it is just a story, and a mostly fictional one at that.

> **Seeker Story**
> The concept that I am not the accumulation of my life experiences but consciousness existing uniquely in each moment has been revolutionary! I continue to let go of the story of me and rediscover who I am in each moment. I find that as I continue to release the story of my life and the concept of the continuity of "me," emotional experiences move through me as though I am digesting something, and I resist the habit of attaching a story and history to the feeling or experience. Without the continuity provided by a story, each challenging moment just seems to pass and then no longer exists. Embracing this new orientation brings a lightness to even the most uncomfortable of moments. I no longer put myself in a box and therefore am not constrained to the limitations of that box. I feel a new freedom, and within that freedom I continue to discover who I really am, each moment, as I unfold. *There is no "who"*

Emotions and Memories

We've all seen children at play and witnessed how a child can be in the midst of a dramatic emotional outburst one minute, and then be happily playing the next. Adults don't usually get over things so quickly. What is the difference?

Emotions arise. They arise from time to time in all of us—anger, delight, fear, passion, disgust—the whole range of emotions. The arising of emotions is natural and part of life. But emotions are designed to be "flash" experiences; they are meant to arise, serve an immediate purpose, and then subside. Some people live in a chronic emotional state, however. They are angry all the time, or sad or fearful. Sometimes we are affected for hours or days by an emotional state that suddenly overtook us; instead of subsiding, it persists. What is going on here? Why are we different from the child?

As noted, the ego files away memories of all types and degrees of significance. It also links similar memories. In this way, if you have an embarrassing experience, it can trigger recall of earlier, similar instances of embarrassment. In addition, the ego not only links similar experiences, it also takes that family of similar experiences and then draws a conclusion about you. Let's say you dropped something. The ego knows the instances when you have done this before. Out of those instances, it makes conclusions about you and proclaims that "you are clumsy." Now, no one likes to be negatively characterized. Being criticized for an incident ("That was a clumsy move") is different from being characterized with a permanent aspect of self ("You are a clumsy person").

Your ego has made up all sorts of positive and negative conclusions about you, about the world, and everyone you know. "You'll never amount to anything." "Fred has always hated you." "You are so clever." "You can't trust Mary." Your ego, however, is no truth-dedicated scholar or Sherlock Holmes logician in its task of making conclusions. It will draw a conclusion of grave consequence at the drop of a hat on the flimsiest of evidence. Nevertheless, it pronounces its conclusion with the authority of a commandment.

The reason, then, why emotional states do not subside as nature intended is that when an emotion arises, the ego mind quickly launches a story related to the emotion, followed by the chain of such stories and the conclusion it has made about you and others. It is that story that persists and keeps obsessively repeating itself in your mind. The story then keeps the emotion engaged, restimulating it endlessly. We are prisoners of the stories we have created about ourselves and the world.

Seeker Story

About two and a half years into my work on this path, I had a realization one day. Somewhat unknowingly, I had released a huge chunk of the story of me! For years I had been living in the drama of how the suffering of my life, which I blamed on my mother, had left me inadequate, not fully developed, and in a state of perpetual suffering. I had so much anger and grief about this, and a deep self-loathing. I lived and breathed this story throughout my life as I searched for healing.

During my "aha" moment, I realized that I hadn't had any of those thoughts or feelings for some time, in fact I couldn't remember when I'd last had one. I was a little shocked and a lot tickled, as you can imagine. The "when" this change first occurred evaded me, but not the "how." At some point in my spiritual work, I really began to live my life in the moment, not dwelling on the past, but on the spiritual potential of right now. I was learning to not lose myself in over-identification with my thoughts and feelings, but rather to see them for what they are, and allow them to move through me without attaching them to a story. I finally "got the memo" that our reality is created by what we choose to put our attention on and that in each moment I had a choice.

I began to access the part of myself that is Divine, One with all, open to love, and I truly started to love myself and accept all that I am, including all of my imperfections, because in my expanded awareness the personal me shrank to its right size in the cosmic scheme of things. My humanity is a small component of the makeup of me. Knowing this made room for the Divine to move through me, and my life has started to change drastically. There is much more to come. I feel by no means fully arrived spiritually, but I now live with the confidence that the Divine is at work in me, and I am a "yes" to the gift of my life! For the first time *ever*, I am a full YES! For this, I cannot begin to speak my gratitude.

The Burden of Coherence

The most towering achievements and important accomplishments of your life are the negotiated creation of the leading character in the saga of your life and the building of the virtual world in which she lives. As the creator "god" of these virtual entities, however, you have the burden and responsibility to ensure that the character and world behave in a coherent and consistent fashion. Both your character and world are awash in rules, thousands of rules. Whenever you interact with your environment you have to consult a vast memory bank to determine the possible courses of potential action that are "allowed" within the rules of your world and personality.

Maintaining coherence of these creations is a heavy burden, and it consumes an enormous amount of the mental and emotional bandwidth available to us. Only a small amount of awareness is thus available to deal with the real world and real events happening in this moment. Even the smallest actions require that we consult our memories and "rulebook," leaving little time or attention for authentic experiencing. As a result, our responses are often inappropriate and ineffective.

Awakening from the Dream

A significant accomplishment on the road to spiritual awakening is to awaken from the dream, from the delusion of your fictional character and her fictional life in her fictional world. What enables that fantasy to persist is that you have forgotten you are her creator, her author. By this stage of your life, the "writing" process is done automatically without conscious effort. It has become a background function that you put no attention on, like breathing or walking. In your spiritual work, what has to be done is to disrupt the automaticity of that recording and call its accuracy into question. Ultimately, you need to deconstruct your invented character and world.

Fundamentally, and here is the rub, you need to discover that you do not exist. Yes, you read that right. This is not a task for the faint of heart! The biggest investment of your life has been the creation of this mythical "you" in the form of storied memories. You believe this is truly you. Your ego will not be thrilled at you trying to dismantle her. This is a gradual process, akin to therapy, in which you examine the fundamental beliefs about who you are. It takes courage and persistence to erase the storyline and make that character smaller and smaller. It is hard and humbling work. But the payoff is life itself.

What propels this process forward — and gives you the confidence and energy to engage in the difficult work of deconstruction — is the growing emergence of true aliveness within you and the greater freedom to act. Your long-imprisoned true self finally sees the possibility of living again, of authentically encountering and experiencing life. This hunger to live can push you through the resistance into freedom and release you from attachment to the false character.

Living Awake

While you are undergoing this transition from the false self to an authentic being, from your virtual world to the real world, there will be a tug-of-war between the security of the past story and the freedom calling to you. This attachment to the past cannot be trivialized, for it is all you can remember being. But no matter how secure or successful this false life has been, there is a core in you that could never accept this confinement. The bird in the cage wants to be free to fly. Your spiritual teacher will be an invaluable ally in this process as she or he encourages you to have the courage to continue in this transition.

The you that yearns to awaken is more bold and daring than the compromised personality your ego has constructed. The real you craves true freedom. It hungers for spontaneous living, even at the expense of security of identity. Life offers us this perverse choice: You can know yourself (i.e., the character in the story) or you can live spontaneously in freedom—but you cannot have both.

To live spontaneously means to live life as a continuous creation. In every moment you are engaged with life and, in each instant, you can respond from the full range of existence, without being confined by the personality of your invented character. By giving up certainty about what you do or don't like, by giving up your conclusions about how things work, by giving up your opinions about how things should be and who you are, the narrow path available to your invented character transforms into a vast open space for discovery and action. It is true freedom. Are you willing to trade the confines of (faulty) self-knowledge and mindless repetition for that freedom? This is what spiritual awakening offers.

In essence, awakening means giving up your past, releasing that past in order to have an unconfined present. But there will also be one more price to pay for true freedom.

The Once and Future You

Your committee spends a huge amount of time thinking about your future: imagining your dreams and aspirations, what you want, and how you might go about getting it. If you observe your mind, you will see how much time it spends in the future. From what you plan to do tomorrow to how you see yourself in

30 years, the future is a compelling escape for the mind. It is an always-available, 24/7 movie theater of unlimited fantasy films.

These imaginings are the source of much of your motivational energy. Out of nothing, you invent a goal and then dedicate yourself to achieving it. Such imagining enables you to escape the unsatisfying present moment, and it gives you a motivating force for change. But it also creates a tension between what is so at the present time and the desired future state. That is not a particularly healthy way to live; however, this condition is chronic in society today. We accept and expect to live in a state of near-continual dissatisfaction with our present lives and circumstances, holding our satisfaction and happiness hostage to an imagined future. In fact, can you even imagine living in a completely contented state without any wish for future improvements in your life?

Your entire lifetime is spent trying to chase the dreams imagined by your ego. One dream replaces another, achieved or not, but always the dreams are for more than you have now. In this ethos, "now" can never be a satisfying moment. This is what you have been taught since early childhood: to always strive for more, and never be satisfied with what you are and have. It is a societal pandemic to which we all succumb.

Spiritual teachers and schools of awakening have to take into account the culture in which they operate. Any spiritual teacher today has to find a way to pull the student out of the imagined, dreamy future world and into the present moment, into now. There are many techniques and practices for this: "What are you thinking about *now*? What are you feeling in your body *now*?"

Techniques can help, but the biggest obstacle is your attachment to what you want your life to become. When I say you will have to give up your past to awaken, many people will make that bargain. But when I say that to awaken you will have to give up your dreams and aspirations for the future, well, that may be a more difficult choice to make. Let's see if I can make that choice easier for you.

The Future Does Not Exist

The only thing that exists, the only thing that is real, is this present moment. Your memories are fabrications, illusions without substance. They are just stories. The future is just a fantasy, an imagined dream. It does not and will never exist. There is only you here now in this very moment.

Please understand that I am not saying that you should never make plans for tomorrow or schedule ahead. Yes, you can book your vacation for this summer, or plan to graduate from college, or set up a retirement account. But such specific and focused plans comprise only a tiny fraction of the time we spend wandering dreamily in the future.

When I worked as a business executive, I understood that future plans must be based on the realities of the present. But for most of us, future dreams are imagined to escape the realities of the present. If you cannot squarely face the present moment, how valid do you think your plans for the future will be?

In any school of spiritual awakening, much of the work involves pulling your mind out of the past and out of the future so that you can fully experience this moment *now*. When you are able to live in the present moment, you will discover that you rarely need to dwell on the future, and that your previous obsession with the future was only because your ego was terrified of what could happen to you. Truly, you only have control over this moment, (and even then, your control is minimal).

Nothing frightens the ego more than knowing that it doesn't have control.

Spiritual awakening will give you so much more power to encounter life and respond effectively and authentically than if you continue to live in the illusion of a future in which you believe there is some control. I invite you to accept the challenge of living in the present: Commit to deconstructing your past and let go of your fantasized future. I promise you, your life will be unimaginably richer. Find the guidance of a good teacher and the support of fellow seekers and set out on the greatest voyage of discovery any human can make: the journey to the center of you, the journey to the center of creation and the experience of each moment.

Practice Suggestions

Here are some practices that can help you stabilize in the present:

1. Whenever you are relating something about your life history, don't just repeat automatically what you've said many times in the past. Instead, when such an impulse arises, tell the story more operatically, more over-the-top, as if you were orating a great saga. The comedic overtones will help dispel the unconscious automaticity of the repetition and give you more awareness about why you are telling this. This will disrupt the underlying psychological impulse for telling the story.
2. Alternatively, when you catch yourself telling a past story, simply stop and keep repeating the words "story, story, story" until the desire passes.
3. When you catch yourself thinking about the future, check with yourself as to whether this imagining is really necessary at this time. If not (and it probably isn't), keep repeating either "daydreaming, daydreaming" or "obsessing, obsessing," depending on the feeling that is generating the thoughts. The point is to interrupt the mind and bring it back to the present moment.

15

The Ladder of Self-Identity

Spiritual awakening involves a profound transformation in identity. What does that mean? As noted previously, in my schema, there are five levels of a being:
- Acted character (the personality you present)
- Ego (the creator, presenter and arbiter of that presentation)
- Authentic individual (you as this alive, natural being behind the mask of ego)
- True self (your fundamental soul nature)
- Godhead (you as Goddess)

At each of these levels, you express a particular self-identity. Now that you have a better understanding of how you create the story of your life, let's revisit those five levels and see how your sense of self-identity evolves as you move from one level to another. At any given stage of your life, you have a "center of gravity" at one of these levels. You may occasionally jump up or down to a different level for a short period, but you soon return to your customary level. In everyday life, shifting permanently to a higher level is a rare and transformational event.

Please note that in this chapter, I will be discussing only individuals functioning with normal psychological health. There are people whose identities are fragile or fractured or who may lack any stable identity at all. Others may suffer from various psychoses or other mental illnesses. Such issues are far beyond the scope of this book.

Self-Identity as the Ego

Let's begin with the second rung, since this is where most of the population lives. I covered this process in the previous chapter. At this level, you identify yourself as your ego, having lost the connection with the authentic self who created that character. Since you believe you are that egoic character, you think you are acting authentically. In earlier chapters, I introduced the "committee," how you come to see yourself as your committee, and how you can use the practice of witnessing to lift yourself out of that level of self-identification. When lost in the grip of that identification, however, you know yourself only as that.

As noted in the last chapter, the character you created was a compromise between what you wanted to be and what your environment wanted from you. The ego knows that there are some aspects of you that are okay to exhibit to the world and other parts that must be kept hidden. The ego character is constantly adjusting this tension line.

Since your egoic identity knows that some parts of you are okay and some are not, the egoic identity creates a second layer of false persona that she sometimes presents to the world. Almost everyone whose self-identity is at the level of the ego will at times utilize such a false self, and when they do, most people know that they are doing it (i.e., they know they are acting inauthentically). Even though they are presenting a first rung persona, they are operating on the second rung of the ladder of self-identity because they know they are not the false persona that they occasionally present to others. However, they actually do believe they are the ego (committee). Of course, they cannot see this; they would not say, for example, "I am my ego." They would just say, "This is me," and only we on the outside can see that she is actually living as her ego.

At this second rung, the ego can perform your public persona occasionally or a lot, as one unvarying character or as a multitude of somewhat different characters. You retain the knowledge, however, that you are a separate self from those characters. But what most of us call "me" is the ego identity, as expressed through the committee, and the authentic self (third rung) is nowhere to be seen.

Self-Identity as the Character Created by the Ego in Your Life Story

At the bottom rung of the ladder of self-identity stand the people who have lost the memory that they are the ego who exhibits the public persona they are living as. Hence they now believe they *are* that persona. This makes them twice removed from their authentic self.

People who live at this level are constantly performing, as best they can, as their ego-created character. They identify themselves as that character and have no idea that they are acting a performance, day in and day out, year after year. When that character must suffer in the plot lines of her drama, the person suffers. When the plot requires joy or confusion or pain or brilliance or any other characteristic, the performer dutifully mocks up those expressions. I say "mocks up" because all of this is inauthentic and unreal. Even powerful emotions are performed more than felt, according to the needs of the story.

Of course, all this is unconscious to the performer (whose creator has ceased to exist in the mind of that person). She believes she is really feeling those expressions. She believes she is that character. To someone who is operating on a higher rung of the self-identity ladder, this may seem like madness. Perhaps it is. But it is socially acceptable madness. If a person thinks she is Marie Antoinette or Cleopatra, we would surely commit her to treatment. But if she is acting "normal" as a believable character, we accept her deception.

In fact, we go much further than mere acceptance. Since most of us are sometimes performing as an inauthentic personality in our dealings with others, we turn a blind eye to others who are giving us a false front, lest we be called out for our own deception. We are part of a huge web of conspiracy. "I won't tell on you if you won't tell on me." Our children learn that we expect them to create such a character and develop a measure of competency in her exhibition. Parents and role models are constantly giving children clues about how they want the child to behave and reward them when they are successful in adapting to that role and punishing them when they do not.

Not all children get trapped at this most basic level of the ladder. The majority make it to the second step. As we have already discussed that level, let us move on to the third rung on the ladder of self-identity.

Self-Identity as an Authentic Person

Listening to your committee is only one way of knowing, and a pretty poor one at that. There are much deeper ways of knowing and living than are available to your ego. The practices in this book are intended to be helpful in this regard to enable you to sense those deeper levels.

Similarly, your physical body has more authentic and natural ways of living than can be expressed by the committee. Sad to say, most bodies, a wonderful gift from nature, are confined and limited to what the committee can imagine and permit. We "tame" and "domesticate" our bodies until they are a mere shadow of their former glorious creature-ness.

With consistent practice, most of us at the second rung could make the climb to the third rung of authentic living, which represents a high level of individuation. Few make the attempt, however. This is a pity, because living authentically is so much more vital, healthy, satisfying, and joyful than what is possible when living as the committee.

As you learn the "feeling state" of authenticity, deeper levels of knowing appear, such as intuition and direct knowing without thought. You also develop the ability to go with the flow of life, to ride its wave, rather than flail about as an ego. You become wiser, calmer, and much more present to each moment.

Few people reach this level, though many aspire to it — or at least aspire to it in dreams and imaginings. For most people, breaking through to authenticity takes hard and courageous work. If we reared our children in a way that encouraged their authentic expression of life from the outset, rather than conditioning and regimenting them, perhaps this third rung would be the rule for our population, not the exception.

The third rung can be a very satisfying level at which to live. Do not confuse it with spiritual opening, however. It represents a high level of psychological functioning, but you have not yet entered the spiritual domains.

Seeker Story

I had been working with Richard for about a year and was committed to a daily meditation practice. Late one afternoon I was meditating at home in front of my altar. I had been feeling lost and confused, so I asked wholeheartedly for guidance, for Spirit to reveal herself so I could better trust my journey of following a spiritual teacher and moving beyond my resistance and ego-bound identity. After spending some time in deep meditation considering "what else is there," I opened my eyes and softened the gaze so that nothing was in sharp focus. Soon a bright golden and green light enveloped the goddess figurine on my altar. Her mouth appeared to smile slyly and the scene shifted as if a curtain opened, revealing a dimensional depth that extended several feet backward into space in a colorful multiverse. My eyes viewed what appeared to be this new dimension and the everyday dimension existing right next to each other at the exact same time. I also noticed sensing a sexual arousal in the lower area of my body that extended upward. This sweet and gentle energy moved in waves up my body and settled in my heart.

During this same window of time, I also experienced a sensation of information cascading rapidly into my consciousness. It felt like a download/reboot of my internal operating system. I experienced a remembering and knowing of who I really am and of some larger purpose that had been obscured by my previous life experiences. In the mix was old cosmic information that made no sense to my mind but still somehow seemed right. I saw the essence of Richard and the essence of the other women in our group dancing an ecstatic dance with the Divine Feminine. Our essences appeared as colorful whirling spirit ribbons dancing together in a circular feminine force field of ecstatic energy.

My mind watched this with curiosity and some confusion, yet my inner being received the information with no attachment and a simple deep knowing of its truth. A few minutes later, my partner and young daughter came bounding into the house full of life and excitement and calling my name. As I opened the door to greet them, my love flowed in delight and I was struck by the contrast of this new experience and insight with the mundane nature of everyday life. I felt I had literally become a different person in a matter of about 30 minutes, yet outwardly nothing had changed at all. I had been granted a glimpse into the true nature of reality. My heart burst open and the desire for a deeper connection with spirit, my teacher, my family, friends, and the whole world came into being. This experience initiated me into a new embrace with life, the great mystery, my teacher's heart, and the larger cosmic dance. It left me with a deeper knowing of what we immortal spirit beings are actually supposed to be doing in these tender little time capsules called human bodies.

Self-Identity as the True Self

When you leave the womb and enter this world, you already have many traits that will accompany you throughout life. You have certain traits of individuality, tendencies of behavior, energy patterns, and bodily characteristics that are unique to you. None of this is "learned." It is all co-emergent with your creation. It is more like the skeleton of your forthcoming uniqueness. All the layers of personality that family, society, and life experiences will add to this lifetime have not yet occurred. At this fundamental level of existence, you are primarily potentiality, not actuality. The chapter on feminine personality and essence introduced this aspect of your existence, your unique "flavor" that reveals a hint of your Divine nature. As you grow spiritually and transcend egoic existence, you return to the pureness of this fundamental nature (as an individual).

When you are able to sense and respond to these innate dispositions, you begin the step up to the fourth rung of your identity ladder. It is also the opening that takes you beyond the limits of material existence and the confines of the physical body. This fourth rung, then, serves as the bridge between material, conditioned life and the eternal, unchanging realm of the Divine. You can feel and sense Spirit and its beckoning call to you, but you do not yet sense that wholeness as yourself.

This fourth rung is the domain of the transpersonal. You still exist as an individual entity but are not limited to that identity. In this domain, psychic abilities may manifest. You may experience going back and forward in time or may journey to other places or dimensions. Communication (channeling) with various kinds of discarnate entities may also occur. Though these siddhi abilities are powerful experiences, do not confuse psychic and other paranormal abilities with Spirit, which constitutes a different domain.

Over the centuries, it has become standard fare for religions to produce "miracles," or at least tales of them, in order to validate the power of their gods. Even we educated moderns seem to demand impossible feats before we fully accept religious or spiritual leaders. We must take care not to confuse psychic abilities or white or black magic as "proof" of spiritual power. No magic is required for awakening. Awakening is an already-present potential in all of us. Realizing this potential may require hard work and honest introspection, but certainly not superpowers.

Some spiritual traditions believe that we have a soul nature that accompanies us from birth to birth. Other traditions speak of Karma that builds up over many lives and gets expressed in this lifetime. No particular belief is necessary to access the domain of the true self; however, meditation and other spiritual practices can quiet our thoughts and "lubricate" that access. In our meditative stillness of mind, we can sense beyond this lifetime and see the present moment of life not as an isolated circumstance but part of a current that began far back in time and extends far into the future. With this vaster vision, our actions are much more attuned to the flow of existence, and we see a purpose for us that reaches beyond this lifetime. This life is but one chapter in a long, long story.

At this fourth rung, you the seeker are now far along in your quest for Spirit. Your self-identity, however, is still that of a separate being who is sometimes connected with Spirit. The final step of Divine Union awaits.

Self-identity as the Goddess

Union with the Divine places you at the fifth and top rung of the ladder of self-identity. The separate self has dissolved and you are in alignment with the flow of existence. The next chapters will discuss how this final merging takes place and what it means to live as an Awakened Being.

Practice Suggestion

Here is a practice that can help you drop into deeper levels of being. Slowly speak this meditation daily on arising and/or before falling asleep. You can speak out loud or in your head, whichever works. Some students prefer to speak the meditation into their smart phone and play it back to themselves.

I AM NOT, I AM

I am not this, I am not that, I am
I am not here, I am not there, I am
I am not up, I am not down, I am
I am not in, I am not out, I am
I am not big, I am not small, I am
I am not hot, I am not cold, I am
I am not hard, I am not soft, I am
I am not good, I am not bad, I am
I am not he, I am not she, I am
I am not you, I am not me, I am
I am not was, I am not will be, I am
I am not life, I am not death, I am
I am, I am, I am…..(Repeat ever more slowly and softly until fading into silence or a quiet hum)

16

Creation and You

Traditional spiritual awakening is seen by many teachers and students alike as a development only of consciousness, and most spiritual practice is designed to this end. However, the body can also become en-lightened. How the spiritual awakening of the body occurs is best understood as a product of the energy of creation, and of opening the body to this universal energy.

At all levels of existence—personal, community, global, and cosmic—creation is a constant process. Whether it's you making dinner, new laws being passed at the town council, flowers being pollinated, babies being conceived, or star systems coming into birth, creation is always happening everywhere. Every time you breathe in air, your body changes; something new is created. Change is constant; nothing is static. Even the rocks and planets change. Old forms yield to new forms. Your own blood cells are completely replaced every few months.

During the very, very brief lifespan of a human, many things seem to remain unchanged, but that is an illusion of time. Nothing stays as it was. Spiritual sages throughout the ages have understood this, but conventional consciousness does not fully grasp the reality of change.

The limited mind of the ego is on a never-ending quest for security and predictability. It is constantly trying to hold on to what it likes for as long as possible and remove itself from what it doesn't like as soon as it can. Consequently, it is always trying to ascertain some semblance of desired stability amidst the chaos of existence. It seeks order, predictability, and sameness. It is happier when it is in control of the pace of change. In the grip of these preferences, it tends to overestimate solidity and stability and under-perceive the extent of change that is taking place.

One result of this is that the ego overemphasizes the separateness and unchanging nature of the body, thinking that it is entirely distinct from the constantly changing environment around it. Aside from the human functions of breathing in air and swallowing food and water, we tend to think we are like a castle with walls. Nothing gets in or out without our permission, or so we believe.

Energy and Matter

Most of us learned in school that matter and energy are interchangeable (remember $E = mc^2$?) and have the same fundamental nature. Like ice and water, we think of matter as a kind of frozen energy. We tend to imagine that energy flows, but matter is solid.

This will be a useful analogy as we look into the nature of the body. Mostly we think of the body as matter: a bunch of water, tissues, and bone surrounded by a flexible package of skin. However, energy is being created and consumed in our body every minute of our lives. Food is being digested and chemically changed into energy. Nerve cells are constantly sending electrical signals. Cells are in regular communication (energy) with surrounding cells and, of course, they are dying and reproducing.

Many spiritual traditions postulate that we have both a physical body of matter and also an energy body. Much of Eastern medicine makes use of this distinction. Whether the energy body is read as auras, adjusted by acupuncture, or regulated by special diet and exercise such as Ayurveda, yoga, and qigong, this energy body is seen as essential for our vitality, health, and well-being. Certain traditions see this spiritually-based energy (*qi, chi, or ki; mana, prana, kundalini*) as a source of great power and have techniques to develop it. In my teaching, I consider the physical and energy bodies to be inextricably interlinked, and my spiritual practices are intended to benefit this combined unit.

Certain traditions postulate other levels of embodiment: psychic, subtle, gross, etheric and so on. Again, I treat these all as an integrated whole. There are many belief systems about the body and healing, from Western allopathic medicine to Eastern medicine to spiritual healing and other beliefs. Similar debates arise over the competing worldviews of mechanistic science, which posits the independence of objects, versus many religious beliefs, which proffer an entirely different view of the universe. One key question in these debates is the relationship between matter and consciousness. In my work, I do not enter into these debates or have any particular insight to offer outside the context of spiritual development. The views I express in this chapter do not come from study of the body or healing modalities or grand theories of the universe. Rather, they are based on what I and other spiritual seekers have undergone during our awakening processes. Also, my teaching is solely for the purpose of spiritual awakening and should not be used as advice concerning the healthy functioning of the body. I do not advocate the existence of "spiritual healing" nor deny such a possibility. As such, I could be considered an "agnostic" in this regard.

Key to understanding the functioning of the energy body is that it is not a self-contained, separate thing from the outside environment. It is not *your* energy; it is energy you are exchanging with the environment. Bodily well-being depends on how you utilize the energy that permeates the space around you. We'll discuss this more in a moment, but first, let's consider the cosmic level.

Existence before Existence

Can you imagine what existence was like before the creation of the universe? Before the big bang (or as stated in the biblical tradition, before God created the heavens and Earth), what was there? Science is only now venturing into that mystery, but ancient spiritual traditions have told of such a time. Many fully realized adepts are able to access a dimension of timelessness and unity. All our lives, you and I have dwelt in a universe of distinctions and constant change. Can we really imagine an era previous to that?

Consider if you can an eternal, unchanging sameness in which no separate thing exists, only oneness, everything-nothing. It would be meaningless to speculate about size, whether as small as a dot on this page or as large as a trillion universes, because this would be a time before the creation of three-dimensional space. Space did not yet exist. In fact, neither did time, for when nothing changes, there is no time. In this—let's call it a primordial universe—there is only an eternal unchanging sameness. In this alternate universe, there is no such thing as creation; it only "is." But then one day an urge arises, a Divine intention to move, to make something happen—in other words, an impulse for change. For change to occur, however, there has to be space in which to move, so that space has to be created. Then the space has to be populated. For that to happen, "things" have to be brought into existence, objects that differ from one another so that they are distinct. With space and change, we now also have the movement of time.

It is not important for our purposes to speculate on how this came about or why, but it is important to register that today we live in a universe filled with countless objects of different qualities, forms, and composition in which change is constant. Therefore, in our universe must be an impulse for creation, for evolution. Without such an impulse, energy, or Divine intention, our universe would not exist, nor would we. Dare we call it a "desire" for change, an impulse that powers the movement of the universe? This creative energy of the Divine moves the universe and everything in it. I call it "Eros," the energy of creation. This Eros initiated change and has caused creation to persist and grow until today we have a vast universe filled with myriad forms, including us. That energy of creation continues to this day.

There is a dilemma in this scheme of things, though, a dark side of the sameness being broken and things being created that were distinct from other things. Since the beginning of life in the universe, there has been an inherent conflict between self and other. Whether an amoeba, a leaf, a fish, or a human, as soon as there is a distinction between inside and outside, between this-ness and that-ness, any organism that can self-identify and self-regulate has seen the world outside itself as a potential threat. Difference breeds fear, and we humans are no exception. Both in our individual actions and the conduct of human groups, fear is always near, and our most fundamental concern is survival, self-preservation against the dangerous "other." So it has been for billions of years. Life = Fear. We'll return to this dilemma in a moment.

Eros: the Energy of Divine Creation

Divine Eros infuses and powers every particle in the universe, every atom, every star, every tree, and every person. Within our bodies, each of us has our own life force, our personal eros, our will to live, move, express, feel, create, and reproduce. This personal eros is our internalized aspect of the one Eros that powers the universe. It is generated by the combination of our biology and the universal Eros. This energy of Divine Creation is very difficult to describe. It is a felt thing that we sense, not something our mind can understand. In talking about it, we have to use metaphor and other symbolic language to convey the idea. Thus we could say that Eros has a unique vibratory signature or harmonic or, more poetically, it is the music of creation.

To our separated, individuated ego, our internal eros seems to be "ours" and as with our physical bodies, we believe it to be separate from everything outside it. We want to protect it from outside influences, and we want our eros to be obedient to our egoic will and to our creature's biology-based desires.

As a small child, our attention and efforts are focused on finding our uniqueness, our separate self, distinguishing it from the world around us. Whether or not we are born in divine oneness, we are born with a body, and it takes a lot of experimentation and attention to be able to use this mobility device and also to learn what constitutes "me" and what is "not me." Discovering which internal sensations contract which muscles and move what parts of the body is a vast exploration. This is true not only for the physical body of matter, but also for the energy body. Children, like animals, are very sensitive energy readers. An infant seeks to feel the energy signature that she learns is hers, hers as distinct from the energy signatures of the various contents of her environment and distinct from the universal music of creation.

Notwithstanding these efforts, we hear people relate stories from their early childhood when they momentarily lost the bounds of the body and experienced a limitless oneness with everything. Those moments are usually fleeting, and the child soon returns to the principal task of establishing a separate identity. As regards the energy body, these efforts at individuation usually entail a contraction from the music of creation, and the child establishes her energy identity by tensing into her own vibratory frequency and modulation. This energy pattern is unique in each individual. It is not a harmony; rather, it is like static noise. In the same way that a child could look at her physical body in a mirror and say, "This is me," she feels the static vibration that her constrictive effort produces and concludes that this also is an essential foundation of "me."

This identification with a specific energy "signature" is not a conscious conclusion, as we are generally not aware that this is a fundamental aspect of our individual identity. Think of this static as a kind of "white noise" that we notice only in its absence. Should that energy change, we may become uneasy, confused, and vulnerable. A part of our identity foundation has been lost.

Most of us, as we grew up, became successful at creating a barrier between the music of creation, Eros, and the constricted internal force field that we experience as our personal life force, or personal eros. Our bodies are designed, however, to have an energy circulatory system that is meant to be in a constant exchange with the energy field of Universal Eros. When we isolate ourselves and cut off the constant infusion of the energy of Universal Eros, we end up in a kind of malnourished state. We have deprived ourselves of the limitless energy of Creation. We live on the mere scraps of it that get through our barrier. This "starvation diet" of energy has consequences for our consciousness and our physical health.

Our constricted energy field gives rise to all manner of compulsions and neurotic behaviors. The life problems that result from this tension are resistant to psychology's usual "talking therapy" methods. The constriction also makes us more vulnerable when we experience physical trauma. It prevents the traumatic energy from being flushed from the body and renewed by fresh Universal Energy. Instead, the disturbed energy stays trapped and stagnant and erupts whenever a triggering stimulus is present. Anyone who's ever experienced profound emotional release from deep tissue massage techniques, such as Rolfing, will know what I mean.

The process of individuation, which includes a stable sense of "me" — my body (and energy body), my thoughts, emotions, memories, and my habits of life — is essential for the establishment of psychological health. Most adults live in such a state of self-identification. This condition is only a waypoint in the evolution of a human, however, not the final stasis of adulthood. What spiritual training offers are practices to lift you out of that limited identification and transport you to a vaster and deeper sense of who and what you are.

Seeker Story

I remember when I first starting experiencing the energies of Eros moving through my body; it was all very disconcerting. There was the fear that I (my ego) would lose myself and my body to a force greater than me. I was not familiar with such physical intensity outside of a sexual experience, and it took some time to accept. Especially so, because the surges and flooding would come in simple moments of daily life — not at all erotic in the conventional sense.

I still feel like an amateur as the volume gets turned up to another level, or perhaps like a channel being changed, because it's not the same note or flavor being intensified. Each time, it's a completely different experience. And each time I have to be vulnerable and open to this cosmic force in order to experience and ultimately learn to navigate it. I feel like an adolescent teen growing into her new body and learning how to feel comfortable. I'm realizing that embodiment is actually a continuum practice, ever changing...not static at all. I don't "achieve" embodiment; I try to keep up!

Most of my cosmic ecstatic experiences felt like I was an instrument — either being tuned or being played. In fact, sometimes live music being played by very conscious people with love and reverence would resonate in my body, and I could physically feel each note being played. At first, it felt like my body and especially my chakras were being tuned to the frequency of a universe: one song, *The* Song. It is the most delicious feeling!

I have also had the experience of being played as an instrument by my loving partner, sometimes without even any physical touch. His mere intention in his hands slowly waving a few inches off my body would create a harmony or song that we could create together. At these times I was completely surrendered to my body for the creation. It was not something that I was intending or trying to create — I just surrendered. Add to

> this the physicality of lovemaking and you can imagine the places we traveled out of consciousness. Lately, there are also intense energetic surges that I receive when my body is relaxed—without any (perceived) stimulus causing it. I'm going to practice opening to receive these as well and will let you know how they manifest, or Womanifest.

Spiritual Awakening as Eros

I've noted throughout the book that spiritual awakening involves a radical transformation in identity. Such is the case for your physical/energy body as well. In conventional consciousness, your senses are tuned to your internal life flow, the small personal eros, your unique energy "signature." As your spiritual practices move you into deeper realms of being, something starts to change. You begin to come into more and more attunement with the Divine Universal Eros. You sense it and, as you sense it, you instinctively want to open and move in harmony with it. If you allow this movement, your body itself, in both its physicality and energy matrix, begins to be infused with this spiritual energy. The exchange of energy between the body and Universal Eros increases. Your very molecules come alive with spiritual presence as your barriers to Eros diminish and your full circulation with Infinite Divine energy is restored.

In opposition to this hunger for attunement with Divine Energy, when your individuated, constricted energy barrier lessens, your ego interprets this as a threat and tries to restore the field to which the ego is accustomed. The encouragement of a spiritual teacher will be a great help to you in trusting the reordering of the energy field so that it comes into greater attunement with the Universal Eros. The more you can relax into this transformation, the more your body will open to spirit and begin to "sing" the music of creation rather than continue to manifest its accustomed static.

Spirit and matter, which were heretofore separate, begin to merge more and more, each informing the other of their two domains until they become one unified Spirit/Matter field. This is the spiritual awakening of the body. It is the uniting of the personal eros with the Universal Eros, the life impulse of the separate human coming into harmony with Spirit/Eros. It is not only your consciousness that becomes the one consciousness, but the body itself awakens to its Divine Nature and integrates into the Oneness of Creation.

As women's bodies are naturally attuned to creating life, they can more readily surrender to the sacred energy of creation, the Universal Eros. Their bodies instinctively sense it and accept it as the natural condition of existence. The separate, individuated energy field of static was never a place that the feminine felt at home; no, it was a compromise for living that she had to bear. When women discover that the restriction can be released and they can surrender to the song of Divine Creation, this is music to their ears (excuse the pun).

One unanticipated benefit of opening the body to the full flow of Eros can be greatly enhanced sexual pleasure. When a child is establishing her state of energy contraction, one reason they do so is because the tensioning can produce pleasurable physical feelings or diminish uncomfortable ones. Then, when they reach a sexually active age, they utilize that learned formula "contraction = physical pleasure" and try to contract and tense up to experience this newfound source of pleasure. Thus, a new formula gets established: "contraction = orgasm." But when Eros is flowing, pleasure comes from a new source: opening and expansion—the greater the expansion, the greater the pleasure. Expansion offers much greater potential for growth (all the way to infinity) than does contraction, and new levels of orgasmic pleasure can be reached.

In sex, the feminine is naturally oriented to opening and expansion, so the effort to achieve sexual pleasure and orgasm through contraction works against her natural flow. It can be done, but it takes focus and effort. On the other hand, receiving sexual pleasure and orgasm through opening to the flow of Divine Eros aligns with her natural bodily instincts, and orgasm can be a more organic and full-bodied experience, and more intimate and loving as well. This phenomenon is another reason for my advocacy in an earlier chapter on the benefits of using sex as a tool for awakening.

For men, the transformation from constriction to Oneness is much more difficult than it is for women. A man's body does not have the energetic attunement to Creation that a woman's body does. Additionally, men live much more in a symbolic, representational world inside their heads. Ancient tantric paths have recognized this for centuries. An Awakened Woman can perform a great service to men by bringing her Divinely attuned wholeness into intimate, loving embrace with his body, filling it with the music of creation. In this love and trust, the man can begin to accept the loss of identification with his static-filled, contracted field and feel the energy of Creation.

This is an art of sacred healing. I hope you will have the opportunity to offer this love gift and bring your man into the awakened state to join with you in the sacred Dance of Creation.

Once established in the bodily-awakened condition, you have not only given yourself an immense gift, but you may also possibly influence the evolution of the universe. Since life began billions of years ago, physical existence has meant living in fearful conflict with the environment and the never-ending energy of

Creation. But now, in an evolutionary breakthrough of incalculable significance, by awakening the body to its Divine state, the fundamental condition of fearful existence is able to change. Isolation of the bodily self ends, and the universe evolves with a new expression of relatedness. The awakened body knows itself to be one with all existence, not separate, and so the fear of survival becomes less of an impediment to fully awakened living. We know ourselves to be one instrument in a great orchestra under Divine direction, and the now-attuned body willingly accepts its role in the never-ending music of becoming. Spirit and matter are truly joined as one. In this unified state, Love becomes the governing expression of the Awakened Soul.

Practice Suggestions

One meditative practice to further the attunement of the personal and universal Eros is to sit in a quiet place and focus your attention on how your body feels.

1. What sensations is your body registering? Take time to be still and keep noting what the body registers, and continue this until you have a very complete registry of what the body is experiencing while you sit there. (You could also do this practice while lying down, as long as you can stay awake.)
2. Feel the vibration rate of your body. It will feel like a very low electric current or perhaps a "hum" of some kind. Feel it as deeply as you can. How does it feel? Is it pleasurable or uncomfortable? Do you have any emotions about it? Note if it is constant or if it varies. Is the variation regular or is it more complex, like music? Is there any place in the body where you can't feel it? If so, can you open those parts to the flow of energy? Continue until you have a vivid sense of how energy is moving in your body.
3. It is very important when doing this exercise that you disregard all information your mind has been taught about the body and energy flow, for example, the idea of kundalini or concepts about chi or chakras. Your body is unique and the flow of Eros will not be limited by the mind's imagined "rules." Just feel; don't think or try to imagine the flow.
4. When you are completely settled into sensing the body's energy flow, begin to feel the energy vibration of the environment around you: in the air, ground, and physical surroundings. Notice whether you feel it as one uniform vibration or if different objects have different vibratory signatures. As you did with your body, see if you can feel whether these vibrations are constant or have regular patterns or other more complex rhythms. Continue until you have established a full sense of the energies around you in

all their variations, all the neighboring signatures of eros. Take all the time you need for this.
5. Return to your body and again feel its full energy patterns along with the other active vibrational movements in your environment. Now, see if you can bring the internal and various external eros patterns into one harmony. This may take some time. Keep going and, like a musical conductor, bring all the separate instruments into one orchestral movement. One song. As you get more and more into attunement, you may find that your energy increases and the flow quickens. You may also experience more clarity, expansiveness, and a feeling of no boundaries. Continue to feel this boundary-less, cohesive, internal/external attunement until your body tells you it is time to end the exercise. As with any other physical learning experience, the body will be more easily able to do this with further practice. Eventually, we want to reach the state where the separate self and personal eros fall away and there is only the oneness of existence and the flow of universal Eros, which is you.
6. When beginning this practice, allow 30 minutes or so. As you gain experience, your body will know when to end.

17

Love that Knows No Limit

The spiritual practices I've outlined have an intended consequence. They serve to open your heart of love. We noted earlier that spiritual awakening involves a radical transformation in identity and relatedness. Awakening as Consciousness and as Eros profoundly transform our identity, our sense of who we are. Now we turn to relatedness, our relationships with others, to address our awakening as Love.

Most of us have feelings of love from time-to-time for this person or that object. But while we often say that we love someone or something, the actual feeling-current of love in the body and emotions (and I'm not talking lust here) is more rare and fleeting. Personal love has a focus: "I love ____."

In truth, such love is often self-serving, but that observation is a huge topic in itself and a digression that we need not delve into for our purposes. Suffice it to say, most of us will claim to have loving feelings, some more often and more deeply than others, but we have to admit that most people are pretty miserly in sharing their love. As a result, few people feel truly loved by us, and we feel truly loved by only a few people. Or maybe there is no one at all we feel genuine love for or from.

The love that is spoken of in spiritual terms is of a different order. It is the agape that you read about in religious and spiritual texts. In Christian mystical contemplation, the love of Jesus/god is the defining characteristic. In Sufism, love of the beloved (god) is the motivating power. Among the various Hindu traditions, Bhakti yoga, the path of love and devotion, is by far the most followed.

This kind of love is more selfless and generous. It is completely different from biology-based love. We are animals, mammals, and we can feel what we would call love for our mates and children, family members, and others closest to us. This is natural and necessary for us to thrive in this life. Agape, or selfless spiritual love, originates from a different dimension of existence.

Many spiritual paths depend on formal practices and rituals for their power. Other paths, such as the ones noted above and the path that I teach, focus on opening the heart to infinite love. In these heart-centered paths, the love shared between the seeker and adept is a mighty "engine" that sweetly powers the student's opening to the more infinite and intangible Divine Love. Their relationship is a passionate embrace in spiritual love, and from that fiery center, the student can let her love expand until one day it will encompass the universe.

Through the student's devoted love for her gurudeva and by using heart-centered spiritual practices, our fearful hearts begin to soften and open, and we find that we can offer love in a broader range of circumstances. It can physically feel as if our hearts are actually expanding in our chests. People and things to which we were previously indifferent, we now feel compassion for and perhaps share what pains and joys they experience. The encounter with life is more precious and tender. The more we practice this opening of the heart, the love we feel encompasses more and more of life.

There is a curious aspect to both romantic and spiritual love that we all may have experienced at one time or another. When we surrender to love, all of our attention and energy flow toward that which we love, to the beloved, not to ourselves. The greater the love, the less attention we have on our separate self and life. The fire of love consumes us; we become that fire and lose our egoic self-absorption. If the fire is hot enough and if we surrender completely, our separate ego-self can be annihilated. Only our love remains. When this happens in romantic love, this surrender can put us in a vulnerable position, for if that which we so desperately love were to be lost, we too would be lost. We would be left with nothing. Many of us have experienced such a heartbreaking loss. So we naturally fear "losing" our self to the power of love and therefore hold back to resist its great power. But agape, spiritual love, is different in this regard. That which we love is eternal and is (potentially) always present.

At some point, this Love begins to transform from being a feeling to having a presence itself. It becomes less of a verb, an action happening, and feels more like a noun, something existing in its own right. We are tapping into that quality of existence. The Star Wars films introduced "the force," as in "May the force be with you." It was said to permeate the universe and bind it together, and events that happened far, far away could be instantly felt by someone sensitive to this binding energy.

The Love that is the essence of the universe is like that. It exists everywhere. It truly is the ocean in which we swim. We are not the originator of it, as we are with the more familiar personal love. No, our role is to open to it and allow it to fill us and move through us. A friend of mine is a singer, and she related the other day that a song came to her fully formed, which she then gave voice to. Her statement was "The song sang me." It is this way with the Love that is the substance of the universe. It loves through us. We are its channel and speaker.

Seeker Story

I am sinking into my body and into the earth in my meditation. As I drop down I am aware of a heavy stillness as the talk of my mind recedes. I am feeling something like a field or a flow of energy that comes through me, through my heart and flowing out into the space around me. It is an overflowing fullness of abundance; a sense that there is so much love available, that I can awaken from the illusion of deficiency and the feeling of separation from Source that make love feel finite. My love could easily envelop the Earth. And yet, the love is not mine. It is a fabric from which everything is made and of which I am made and woven together with everything around me, and everything that has ever been and ever will be. In this moment I do not feel desire, but I can feel the field of lovingness from which a desire could arise.

I have been the pull of different fragments of ego personality emerging to meet external circumstances. Now, when they are speaking, it is as though a conversation is happening above the surface of the ocean while I am submerged below, deep and far away. Underneath, the field of love is still and silent. When it speaks, it is as though I am rising out of water, and the words and energy move directly and clearly through the air.

The words "beloved" and "devotion" are coming to me now. I feel a contemplation in which these two words are the subject and the object. I hold the frequency of these words in my heart as I behold the world. Could I behold everything in beloved devotion?

Our experience of this Love does not depend on the presence of a single object; therefore, it cannot be lost. Like the air we breathe, it surrounds us. This Love is infinite and eternal. Our opportunity is to become its servant, to be a vehicle through which it can express itself in our material world. We are not the chooser of who or what to love or when; rather, we are its steadfast messengers.

It is also our nurturer, our sustainer. We never need to live a moment without this Divine Love. This Love is what feeds and nurtures us. It never judges us and is always forgiving of us. We have only to be willing to receive it, to drink from this bountiful well of Love. We allow ourselves to be immersed in the ocean of love, and from our fullness we can offer it to others.

By surrendering to this mission, we transcend even the role of its carrier and merge with it to become that Love ourselves. It fills our bodies and minds. Rather than being an on-off focused transmitter of occasional love, our heart fills and fills with Love and, at some point, it explodes to encompass the universe. Like the sun and its light, we radiate Love to all, without preference or distinction. It is free to all who can feel it. We are not a "do-er" of lovingness but have become Love itself. Whereas before, we were a person who expressed love and acted lovingly, now we *are* Love. We are Love infinite and everlasting.

This is what is meant by the awakening of the heart.

This could be you. You have only to surrender to Love.

The Practice of Love

The opening of the heart can happen gradually as a natural process aided by the various practices noted in the book. There are a number of more structured practices that also serve this end. For example, in Buddhism, *metta* and *tonglen* meditation are used to increase compassion. Resources that describe these meditations are easily found online and in bookstores. Though compassion is a somewhat different expression of the heart than the opening to Love that I teach, meditations to develop and increase compassion can further this end.

Receiving practice: If you can remember ever receiving unconditional love, or something close to it, a worthwhile practice is to sit quietly and relive those moments. Feel what it was like to receive the warmth of such love. How did your body feel? What emotions were you feeling? Allow yourself to be present to those moments. Feel your innocence and openness. When you have felt that fullness, see if you can magnify it and allow it to overtake you to the point that it feels as if your heart will break from the fullness of the love you are receiving. As you repeat the practice, you may feel your capacity to receive love expand to the point where you, the receiver, and the love flowing to you are one and the same, that there is no separation from you the receiver, the giver of that love, and the love itself.

Offering practice: The second practice is the reverse of the first. Recall the deepest, most unconditional love you can remember giving, and re-experience those feelings. Recall all such moments and let yourself feel them again. Look to see if you can magnify the feelings—in your body, in your emotions, and in your heart. Expand them as far as you can. As with the first practice, perhaps one day the boundaries between you and the object of your love, and with Love itself, will blur and merge.

In addition to these meditations, you can practice love throughout your day. You may believe that you need to have certain conditions in place before you can open your heart and share your love or compassion. For most people, time and space for love come last, after all our "pressing needs" are satisfied. We want our chores done; we want our grievances with the person first aired; we want to feel emotionally safe. The list of conditions that have to be satisfied before opening the heart can be long indeed. I ask my students instead to put love first. Don't act until you can feel your love. If you are angry with someone, for example, don't immediately express the anger. Wait a bit until you can feel your love for that person and then communicate your anger from that more openhearted place. This practice can be done in any setting: at work, at home, with friends. The love can be present, though the way it is expressed may be tailored to fit the cultural circumstances and context.

Over time, you will learn that your heart is not as fragile as you believed and also that you can feel love in a broader range of circumstances. You will see that you need not be stingy in its expression. As a life practice, your love can grow to such an extent that it would be rare if you could not feel love for someone in your midst.

Your heart has always wanted this. Most of us were taught that love must be limited to very few people. For our young hearts to make this closure bearable, many of us rechanneled that blocked energy flow and put it into judgments, evaluations, and opinions about others. The energy of love is only too happy to be rerouted back to its proper function. By doing this, you relearn what you instinctively knew as a young child: Love is more important than judgments.

18

Merging with Spirit

Consistently performing the practices described in the previous chapters will bring you, the seeker, a long way on your journey of awakening. Using these practices, you can note what your ego mind, your committee, wants and at the same time you can see what situations call for. Over time, you will establish the habit of choosing what is needed over what your little ego-mind desires. Your thoughts no longer loiter in the past or future or in storied fantasies of who you are. Instead, you sense what is happening in this moment. Your body is in harmony with Eros, and pulses with the energy of creation. You are learning to live authentically and spontaneously. Also, you offer yourself as a contribution to Love, as a heart gift of service and compassion. As the practices continue, you will establish greater and greater distance from the yammering of the committee and will no longer get caught up in its insistencies and inconsistencies. You become very, very present in this moment. You are calm and centered and able to respond to life from a place of pure creation, not from conditioned and learned responses. In this space, life can be wonderful and wondrous.

But there is another realization awaiting you. This final discovery will bring you face-to-face with the essence of your spiritual dilemma: the illusion of the separate self. With the clarity available from your newfound perspectives, you can now face the essential problem of existence: the idea that you are a separate self who is at odds with life, with existence, with Spirit.

Separation = Fear

The crux of the delusion that characterizes ordinary life is this: We see ourselves as a body and mind, a creature, separate from the rest of existence, cut off and alone. We first looked at this in the chapter "Creation and You." Existence is divided into self and other, inside and outside. From that disconnected place, we see the environment around us as uninterested in our well-being, sometimes even hostile to our needs. We live as if we are in dangerous territory, with only a few souls who care even in the slightest about our welfare.

In that bleak situation, the task falls to our ego to ensure that we survive. Long ago, we abdicated to that inner entity the responsibility to act as our "department of defense." Of course, our little ego had not the slightest idea of how to do that job, but nevertheless loyally assumed the burden, and she has been overwhelmed ever since. The human ego is simply not designed to hold such a great accountability.

Inside of this egocentric view of reality, all of life is lived as a struggle between what the ego strives for in order to further our security and happiness, and the circumstances that the world presents to it. Life deals us certain cards, but we want other cards. "I want" versus "what is" is the struggle we live every day.

As you dig deeper into the true nature of reality and the depth of yourself, a new reality emerges. In this new reality, you come to see that you are far vaster than the small mind-body you believed formed your personal identity. You discover you are omni-connected with all that exists, that you are the oneness below the apparent diverse appearances. With this expanded version of Self, the fear of survival subsides, and with it the need for the ego to struggle against life and your need for the ego to act as your survival director.

The spiritual practices described in the preceding chapters, when done in concert, gradually (or sometimes very suddenly) allow that new version of reality to emerge. Slowly, slowly, slowly, they encourage you to relax the grip of self-contraction in order to discover the quiet depth that is truly you. Your patience and persistence in the spiritual practices are rewarded, and more and more glimpses into the true nature of existence are given to you.

> **Seeker Story**
> There is a field, and it is the light of a transmission. When I joined our Circle, I was in a very shattered place. I was in the middle of a very difficult and painful divorce, and there was no part of me that did not feel broken or inadequate in some way. From this depth of pain, I was very open and vulnerable, especially to energy. I realized in my many individual and group meetings with my teacher that a "Transmission" was happening. Something very moving and invisible was happening whenever I was in the presence of this great teacher, guide, guru. And I realized there was a field that began to expand over time.
>
> I had a situation where I moved into a rental home where I did not feel completely safe. I had broken up my family by leaving my husband, and I seemed to have lost my material footing. As I was experiencing this great chasm of loss, a burglar came and everything of any value was taken. Someone had

> broken into the house in broad daylight and taken our family TV, computer, cell phones—all of our electronic anything was gone—and I was in no financial position to replace what was taken. Then, months later, my minivan was broken into and thieves took all of my work tools.
>
> Teacher did an amazing process with me. He came over and he walked around the perimeter of my home as if to shine a protection over every boundary of my little rental property. Together we visualized a light, as if you could actually see a golden light emanating from the property. From that day forward, I began to feel more and more safe, until I felt completely comfortable and protected in my little home.
>
> Many Circle meetings are held in my home, and it is as though with every meeting, a little more love comes into this space energetically. At first I could only feel the energy with our teacher, but as we have grown and deepened and come together as a group, I feel the field extending not only through the transmission of energy that he brings, but it is also starting to come through as a group, and the energy has taken on a different flavor and has expanded. If you could put glasses on and literally see the light, I would imagine that my little house is like a beacon of light in the neighborhood. This light for me is a transmission of love, of divine protection, and a beacon of light. I love to have the group in my home because I truly feel the energy and transmission continue to grow. There is a field, a real and tangible field—I'll meet you there.

You Are the Flow of Existence Itself

Gradually, you learn to stop fighting with "what is" and instead "go with the flow." I call it surrendering to "what's so." You sense that there seems to be purposefulness to the universe, that it is evolving and each particle (including you) is part of that evolutionary intent. You feel what existence is calling for from you, and you start to cooperate with that call.

When you surrender to life as it is, living becomes not only easier, but also more fulfilling and true. You feel you are on the right path and that your actions are in harmony with a greater purpose. You learn that living this way does not impoverish you or drive you to painful martyrdom, but offers you more fulfillment and ease. You find that you matter and that your existence is an essential—I repeat, essential—part of the grand universal design. You know you make a difference.

Ending the argument with life as it presents itself to you is a great breakthrough. Now, instead of fighting against the forces of existence, you can be buoyed and carried by them. Along with this transformation of how to live comes an accompanying transformation in the right use of will. In the past, your personal will was arrayed against the other forces of life. It was your will that had you strive for what you wanted against the (believed) universal forces of indifference and opposition. In so doing, you were contending with the billions of other personal wills for meager scraps of life.

Women are so much more able than men to surrender to the natural flow of life. Males tend to be much more identified with their will than females are. In today's world, will is highly honored and encouraged in males. In truth, with that puny will, we men are acting much like Don Quixote, myopically battling windmills. Mostly, we live with frustration and fear. In contrast, women are more naturally attuned to accommodating the flow of the universe. Mothers, especially, know the futility of placing their will against what life is demanding of them. A helpless infant needs what it needs, regardless of whether the mother is exhausted, overwhelmed, ill, grumpy, or wishes to be relieved of her burden. She must surrender her will again and again and again. A baby is a fierce spiritual teacher

As you spiritually mature, you more readily sense what the Divine wants with you, and your inner "homing instinct" beckons you to harmonize with that superior wisdom. You make the shift from my will to Thy Will. Once you have surrendered in service to the Divine Will, your personal will can shift its role from being antagonistic to being purposeful in carrying out that Divine Will. Once you align your personal will to the Divine Will, you enter a state of grace wherein all manner of assistance is available to you. Success is no longer solely up to your little ego, but is empowered by the evolutionary impulse of Creation itself. You have become an instrument of Divine Creation.

> **Seeker Story**
> I had a huge heart opening experience today while walking in the park and experiencing the diversity of humanity. In the midst of the mind-f--- and anger my mental committee was running about how I can't trust or rely on anyone to meet me, see me or love me (as if I can always offer this!), my heart broke open and the information came once again—this is not about the small story of me and my life. It is the story of humanity, and my love, compassion, and ability to see and hold it all is what is needed. What a world I've chosen to be waking up into! My anger gives way to tears and tenderness. I surrender again!

The Incredible Shrinking Woman

Imagine being an artist, a sculptor of stone. You've heard the truism that the sculptor's job is to liberate the figure within the block by chipping away all that is not the figure until only the figure remains. In this view, the sculptor is not creating the figure per se, but only exposing the figure that was always hidden inside the block of stone. The sculptor has the eyes that can "see" the figure beneath the surface of the stone block.

Getting to our spiritual core is somewhat like this process. In Hinduism, there is the Sanskrit phrase *neti neti,* which means "not this, not that." The seeker is encouraged to look at everything she identifies with and to see it as "not me." You are not your job title or trade; you are not your body; you are not your relationships or your thoughts. It is a form of meditation used to help you discover your essential core, the true self, and wean your mind from identification with lesser things.

With this in mind, consider this revision of the scenario of the sculptor who seeks to chip away the superfluous stone in order to reveal its essence. In this case, what is to be revealed by chipping away is the sculptor's true self. For our new scenario, instead of stone, let's give her a big block of ice to sculpt and locate her in Miami Beach in the summer. Our fearless artist chips away at a section of the ice and reveals a part that she feels is truly the self. She has perfectly sculpted it. Then she moves on to another section and chips away until that part, too, reflects her true self. But then she glances back at her first area of work and discovers the section that was formerly a perfect representation of that first aspect of her has melted somewhat. The fine lines are no longer there. So she chips away a bit more at that first section in order to restore the perfection of that aspect of the figure. She then turns to a third section to expose that aspect of the figure, but the other sections are meanwhile melting. With her efforts now at full speed, she works feverishly at one section and then another, and another, all the while chasing to restore perfection to the melting ice. Eventually, she is left standing there with only a puddle of water to show for her efforts.

In the case of the spiritual seeker, she exposes facets of herself and releases (chips away at) the aspects that no longer represent her. She does this again and again with other facets of herself. But when she returns to that first facet, she sees still more that she no longer identifies with and can release more of what she formerly believed to be truly herself. And so it goes. More and more, you see that less and less is really the essence of you. *Neti neti.* And then you let go of more. What you believe to be the essential core of you gets smaller and smaller until there is nothing left but a tiny point in space, and then even that goes "poof." And with that poof, the infinitesimally small point that was you becomes one with all of existence. There is no longer any self and other, only is-ness. You have now entered the Eternal Infinite Oneness (EIO).

In this state, words fail completely. It can be experienced but not described. Different traditions have different names for it. Buddhists describe it as emptiness, *sunyata,* but the word has also been translated as "openness," "onlyness," and "suchness." In the paradox that this state represents, we could also call it oneness or everythingness. Other traditions may call it one with God. But it is the experienced, felt state that is important, not the words used.

Here you have come to the point of nonduality. Previously, you were a person who wanted to find her authentic self and be in relationship with God, with spirit. You searched and searched until finally you came to the "X marks the spot" on your internal treasure map. There you find that there was no one who was searching; there is only God. The separate you has vanished. Everything that you once were has been lost, sacrificed in order to become everything. You and God have become one and the same. Instead of being a worshipper outside of God, you have merged, and the self that you were has evaporated in the fire of

Divine Onlyness. Or, as the Sufi poet Hafiz said, "I searched for God and found only myself. I searched for myself and found only God."

This awakening can be celebrated, as we do with any birth of new life. You have been born to Spirit. But while we deservedly celebrate that birth, we must also say goodbye to one who has departed. You, as a separate self has died, died along with the dream world that you believed existed. The crawling caterpillar is no more. You now wear the wings of the butterfly, and the freedom of flight is yours.

As consciousness, you are one with the One Consciousness. As love, agape, you are now one with the Love that is the essence of existence. As Eros, you and your body are one with the creative force of life. You are the Eternal Infinite Oneness.

At last, the war between self and other is over. There is only the Divine Flow of Life, of which you are an instrumental and essential aspect. You are one with existence; you are one with Spirit.

You are home.

19

Communion in Union: The Divine Paradox

You have merged with Spirit and abide in the singularity of the Eternal Infinite Oneness. In this realization, you have joined the thousands of mystics who have experienced this domain of reality over many centuries. Many mystical traditions, especially Eastern traditions, have deeply explored this realm. Less investigated is a paradox of relatedness encountered here.

I touched on this in Chapter 17, "Love That Knows No Limit." For there to be love, there must be relationship. Love is an energy shared between beings. It is communal. Yet at the heart of the oneness, we feel that Love and know ourselves to be it.

One of the great realizations of humanity is that the oneness that is the foundation of existence in the universe is the same identity as the individual at her deepest depth. Or, as the Hindus say, "Atman is Brahman."

Here we look further. In the heart of that emptiness, we find not merely an impersonal absolute, but also Love. The phrase made popular by the hippies of the 1960s and '70s actually turned out to be true: "God is Love." As a Divinely realized being, you are also that Love.

> **Seeker Story**
> I was on an Eastern-based spiritual path for the majority of my life. I started meditating when I was thirteen years old at boarding school in England in the Theravadan Buddhist tradition. I found a refuge in Eastern philosophies, as they were a forum for inquiring into the nature of being and mind, which I was very interested in. I continued down this path with various Buddhist teachers until I found this spiritual path, when I was almost forty years old.
>
> Although meditation has been a solid training ground for cultivating the witness, I see clearly now how that practice created a sense of separation between spiritual life and regular life. I thought I only had spiritual experiences when I was sitting on a cushion, or being a good student. When I was introduced into the group that Richard was leading, I was told it was a meditation group. But it did not look like any other meditation group I had ever experienced. In fact, there was basically no sitting meditation at all, or silent practices. What there was instead was an invitation into integrating matter and spirit, Heaven and Earth, body and divinity. This is a path of immanent Awakening, not dependent on any particular postures, mantras, or sitting practices. This is the real deal, being awake *now*, and not hiding behind attachment to a particular dogma.
>
> I have had more spiritual movement in the past three years than the prior 27 combined. I'm a truly more loving, heart-centered person and have found an Awakening of my Eros that has been unexpected and pleasurable. And my spirit continues to feel more and more true freedom. I no longer hide behind the identity of being a "spiritual person," but aim to be awake, embodied, and free. To bring it back to my Eastern teachings, I aim to be a Buddha, not a Buddhist.

There can be no love without relationship, without an "other." Here is the paradox: At the center of existence, we find oneness; we find nonseparation. But at the same time we experience the feeling of love for all others. There is only one, but love requires an "other," yet both feelings are present in the experience of enlightenment.

Together, awakened humans represent a communion of souls in the oneness. In a manner of speaking, all people are one person. As you dive deeper into your depths, this becomes more apparent. All are bound in Love of one another. Oneness in the multiplicity is the paradox that is revealed. This paradox cannot be understood by the mind, but in the heart it is experienced as truth. You and I are one, yet we commune together as lovers, as separate beings. And so it is for all. Let's give the Beatles' prescient lyrics the last word on this topic:

I am he as you are he as you are me and we are all together.

20

Death and the Divine

No book on spiritual awakening could be complete without discussing the matter of death. Therefore, before we move on to the triumphant end of the spiritual journey outlined so far, let us pause for a moment and consider this topic.

Life is hard. Then you die.
—David Gerrold

These two perversities of life, its difficulties and death, provide desperate motives for religion. People hunger for an explanation of why life is so difficult and uncaring, why injustice, evil, and ineptitude seem so prevalent and often rewarded. When faced with drought and plague, illness or economic collapse and war, we long for understanding, with the hope that such understanding will offer some measure of control over our adversity, or at least console us with resignation to our fate.

Life can be good as well as bad, so our concern about life's difficulties, large as it is, pales in comparison with our fear of life's inevitable end: our annihilation. The specter of death hangs over us as a grim IOU that we know one day will be collected. Birth presages a death sentence. Mostly, people avoid thinking about it and give their full attention to living life, not often worrying about death's grim inevitability. Always in the background, however, there the grim reaper sits, and also in the background is our (faint) hope for some solution, our wish for an alternative. The "circle of life" may offer a comforting philosophical context for death, but not when it is *my* life we are talking about.

Religions offer various beliefs to comfort our anxiety about death. One is that only the body dies and the spirit will roam the earth forever. Another is the belief in karmic reincarnation, that we keep being reborn, and reborn, and reborn. Then there is the widespread belief that at death we will be "promoted" to a paradise (or "demoted" to a hellish existence) where we will live forever. Though these beliefs may be sufficient to keep some hope alive, the dearth of evidence of those afterlives keeps the proposition iffy except for the most fervent, unquestioning believers. Nevertheless, people will cling to any hope, no matter how desperate, when the alternative is unacceptable, thereby making them easy prey to the providers of such claims.

Though we may not wish to succumb to fantastical promises for continuation of our existence, science, philosophy, and the intellect have failed to produce an acceptable alternative. Science's conception of a vast, dead, "clockworks" universe in which humans have a speck of fleeting existence is not exactly an empowering or inspiring vision. This reality posited by mechanistic science leaves humans in the unenviable position of being the only species we know of who are intelligent enough to grasp the certainty of their forthcoming annihilation.

Believing that death is unavoidable, science has turned its attention to life prolongation. In the coming decades, technology will permit humans (at least the very wealthy ones) to live a much longer life. If that meant expanding the length of our 20s, 30s, and 40s, many would be delighted to prolong those years. But if going from an expected 90 to 150 merely means a continual decline from today's aged years (110 is the new 90?), that may be less appealing. We should also take a clue from nature, who has been at this game for billions of years and has tested every possible scenario. Some plants can live a very, very long time, but for creatures with mobility, any species that approaches a human lifespan is very rare. Of the terrestrial species, giant tortoises seem to be the longevity champs, but they are barely mobile. A very few birds and some aquatic animals can go past the century mark, but all in all, brief lives are the norm. Species seem to be designed that way. Apparently, nature has learned that it is better to have frequent new software upgrades (new generations) rather than to design creatures that can live indefinitely. If humanity heads in the direction of longevity, we do so at our own peril.

Our human intellect is also powerful enough to grasp the concept of immortality, of existence beyond time. We can also imagine (and envy) a being who is immortal, who is not subject to death and decay. We can then conceive what such a being would be like. In the Abrahamic religions (Judaism, Christianity, and Islam), this being is imagined to be all-powerful, but whatever attributes a society gives to its immortals, they are called gods. Herein is the foundation of dualistic religions discussed earlier in the book. Life is divided into two realms: The first is one of phenomenological changes, including birth and death, the second an eternal realm. Mortal humans dwell in the former and immortal gods in the latter (though those gods are sometimes believed to be able to bestow immortality on humans if they wish, i.e., promoting us to heaven, Olympus or some such afterlife).

Even if we could believe that we will continue in some manner after death, it is *this* life that we are passionately attached to at the moment and wish to continue. "I want to live!" cries our ego. This desperate statement offers a hint that our view of reality may not be as it seems.

The Personal Immortal

People who have awakened spiritually generally seem to have little fear or concern about their prospective death. This is quite a contrast with the general public who, as noted, live in conscious or unconscious dread of death. What is different for the awakened ones that enables them to accept this fact of life?

In conventional life, our sense of self (our answer to the question "Who am I?") would be limited to our body and mind, the latter consisting of our thoughts and emotions. Both the body and mind are decidedly mortal entities subject to decay and, ultimately, death.

Spiritual practices consist of exercises to expand our sense of self by raising awareness of other aspects of our being (the ladder of self-identity). Eventually, the foundation, the seat, of our identity no longer rests in the body-mind but in a very different sense of who we truly are. This expanded conception of self is not a mere idea or intellectual construct. The greater identity is not something imagined, but something known, something actually felt and experienced. This newly discovered identity, in direct contrast with the fragile body-mind, is immortal. It is immortal, and it is also personal. "I am that."

Indeed, the whole effort of spiritual awakening leads us to the discovery of our immortal self. This aspect of our existence was always the case and an always-available knowing; however, we were blind to it. In the midst of the constant activities and challenges of daily living, the quiet subtlety of our infinite nature goes unnoticed. Therefore, most spiritual paths emphasize a simpler, quieter, more contemplative life in order to provide the conditions for this realization.

With spiritual practice, you discover that it is not imagined gods or other discarnate beings that are immortal, but you, yourself, are everlasting. Humans thus have both mortal and immortal aspects of their existence, one foot in the door of each, so to speak. We are paradoxical in this way. Once awakened, you can choose to focus on one or the other. At any moment, you can put your attention on your body and mind and actively live as a mortal. In another moment, you can put your attention on your immortal, infinite foundation and abide as that.

Again, this realization is experienced and known to be true, not merely believed as a matter of faith or philosophy. The enlightened answer to the question "Who am I?" is "everything and nothing," for it is a state of non-separation. You are all that is, has ever been, will ever be, and the emptiness from which all arises. With that realization, the impermanence of the body and mind becomes a matter of little consequence, and you can face their loss with great equanimity and peace. Your responsibility, then, is to find your immortality while you live, and not wait and hope for it after you die. The mystical poet Kabir understood this six centuries ago when he wrote: *What you call "salvation" belongs to the time before death. If you don't break your ropes while you are alive, do you think ghosts will do it after?*

As you are both the Divine wholeness as well as a mortal creature, you have the opportunity to know both realms, and in so doing knit together in one great understanding these seemingly incompatible domains of existence. Through your awarene you can bring them together in a grand union of consciousness, the perishable and imperishable aspects of Being. Through you, the Divine can come to know itself through the eyes of its creation. The formless/everlasting/transcendental can meet the limited/conditional and know the other to be its very Self. Spirit and matter are one; you and God are one, Atman is Brahman.

21

Transcending Ego: Awakening as Oneness

The preceding chapters of Part II have looked at the process of awakening, its various facets, and some spiritual practices to realize the awakened condition. Let us now try to pull it all together. The practices that have been outlined here, combined with the wisdom and compassionate holding of a teacher, can lead you to full spiritual awakening. You *can* become enlightened.

Slowly, you have been letting go of your ego and discovering a vaster you. The initial spark has become a smoldering ember that ignited small twigs of awakening energy, which, in turn, enflamed larger branches until one day you exploded into the awakened condition. Along the way, you experienced moments of this state, increasing in frequency and duration, until one day that state became your permanent condition.

Let's assume you have reached this place of stable wakefulness. What is it like? What have you been working so hard to achieve? What is life like after awakening? As you read, please keep in mind my earlier injunction that no words can do justice to this state. Every experience of it is personal; there is no "official" or universal description. You will truly know it only when you have arrived there, not from reading or hearing the words of an adept or even receiving transmission from them. You will be the first human to step into *your* awakened condition, a place unique in the universe. Nevertheless, perhaps my words will offer hints that will be helpful later in your journey.

The Awakened Condition

The awakened condition is not the same as having momentary glimpses of expanded consciousness, those awesome peak experiences in which for a brief time you experience a great sense of wonder, oneness, divinity, ecstasy, timelessness, spaciousness, or fulfillment. Perhaps the experiences came with the assistance of mind-altering drugs, or in lovemaking, or, conversely, from tragedy or strife. Or maybe you were in nature witnessing a beautiful spectacle, or in meditation or other spiritual practices, or maybe you were doing nothing at all when the peak experience arose.

Many people report experiences like these. If you have had such an experience, it was probably a wondrous moment of your life, and you most likely remember it vividly. Maybe it even changed your life in a profound way.

If you can recall such a moment in your life, imagine this: Remembering that experience, take away the chemical effects from drugs (if any were involved), remove the oxytocin and dopamine high, settle down the surging emotions, and what you have left is a great spaciousness and feeling of timeless connection with all of existence, with a sense of profound sacredness. At the center of it all is a calm, silent, and present abiding. That is the "awakened" aspect of the peak experience.

The Hindus call it *satcitananda* (*sat*, existence or being; *cit*, consciousness; *ananda*, bliss), the experience of Brahman.

Now imagine that awakened experience being potentially available to you at any moment in your life. Imagine that, in the midst of life's hurly-burly cacophony of demands, you could access this state at any time. You could be in rush-hour traffic and it is available to you. Someone could be in your face, very upset with you, and you could access this state. Wouldn't that be wonderful? That is living in the awakened condition. You go about your affairs as you always have, and much of the time you will also be in a state of serenity, limitlessness, and connection. This state is available to anyone who is willing to do the work to get there.

This does not mean that you no longer experience negative and difficult thoughts, emotions, and circumstances. The limited, conditional, creature aspect of you is still alive and active. All the swings of emotions can still arise from time to time. Life can be challenging, awake or not. Given that, how is enlightened living any different from the norm?

The key is that you no longer believe the negative thoughts and no longer consider the feelings to be yours. All those appearances are merely things happening in your environment. They are not expressions of you. We talked earlier in the book about the dance of attention, and how it bounces from object to object. Your familiarity with the awakened conditions means that most of the time you can direct your attention away from the activities of the mind and body and abide in the unity of the awakened condition. You do not get "lost" in your thoughts and feelings.

With this ability to focus your attention, your ego mind (the committee) no longer controls your behavior. You may consult with it from time to time, but you are in charge. Your wisdom

wing have expanded far beyond what that motley crew
er. You accept the challenges and adversities of life with
equanimity, and you have little of the knee-jerk reactiveness that may have plagued you in the past. You are calm.

Emotions no longer have to be held in check. You have access to a broader range of emotions than ever before. Even emotions that in the past you would have felt to be negative, you now see as useful and can express them responsibly and powerfully.

You feel so connected with everything, your family and friends, the trees and flowers, all the creatures, the Universe, and everyone and everything in it. It is all you. You feel that you are living in the experience of Truth, that you are experiencing Reality as it truly is. Without their knowing why, people feel better when they are around you. You have "good vibes." When you focus on someone, they relax. You emit an energy of Love that all can bask in.

You are more feminine than ever, and men and women alike are irresistibly attracted to that energy. You enjoy being a woman and freely offer your life-force energy to the world. You are alive and vibrant in your body and revel in that continuous ecstasy of aliveness. You are grateful to be alive.

What others feel, you also feel. Their joys and sufferings are known to you and felt in your being and body. You wish only for others to be happy, and desire to serve them to the extent you can. You have great compassion for everyone, even people you may have grievances against. You may also feel great sorrow and pain at the current state of humanity and human cruelties and indifference to each other. You experience the truthfulness of the Mayan greeting that is also said as goodbye: "You are another me."

You are a mystery to yourself. "I like this" or "I don't like that" have much less certainty and power than before. You could like or not like whatever the next moment brings, and you are not attached to either feeling. You stand fully in this instant ready to deal with whatever the next moment brings. You have little desire to control things and are content to let the future unfold as it will. This does not mean you are passive and indifferent toward life. On the contrary, you flow with purposefulness and a sense of destiny.

You enjoy life. You understand that though we call this a "state," awakening is actually a stage of evolution of what it means to be human. Just as an adult has evolved further than has a child or teenager, you have reached a stage of evolution beyond "normal" adult life. At the same time, you are still a human with all the emotions, thoughts, and sensations that any person has. What has changed is that you no longer are identified with these experiences.

The More than You, You

In the awakened condition, your life is no longer limited to the personal you. You come to know your transpersonal nature. Existence is a paradox in which you experience yourself as Oneness without separate existence, while at the same time you are a separate creature relating to other separate creatures inside a vast Universe. Whichever perspective you happen to have in the moment, you know you are far, far greater than your body. Perhaps you are able to journey great distances from the body and experience existence from other separate perspectives. Here or there, it is all the same to you.

You live to serve. You are not limited to the selfish grasping of a limited ego mind. Whether or not you have taken a formal bodhisattva vow, you instinctively want all beings to be loved, honored, and cared for.

In the awakened condition, you also experience your eternal nature, and with that knowing of your infinite life, the specter of death loses its terror. Death of the body-mind is no longer a thing to be feared. You and God are one already. No need to wait until death for that to happen.

The Transition Years

From what I've described, you can see how radically different this stage is from the "normal," unawakened condition of humanity, hence the term "radical awakening." The stage of evolution that I am calling the awakened condition does not usually appear overnight (though that can sometimes happen). People typically work for years to reach this state.

The human mind and body do not adjust immediately to this new, expanded condition. Even after you have awakened, you will probably drift in and out of that state for some time to come until you finally stabilize there. It will likely take some years to normalize in this state. Think of these years as similar to your teenage years when you were awkwardly oscillating between the child you were leaving behind and the adult you were slowly becoming. Once awakening materializes in you, you will again have some awkward "adolescent" years while you oscillate between being a fearful, selfish ego and a magnanimous Divine Being, a Goddess-on-Earth.

This period can be disorienting to the newly awakened person, since the two realities of existence—ego-identification and enlightenment—are so radically different. Therefore, notwithstanding any impulse you may have to fly on your own, it will be important to remain in the warm holding of your fellow seekers and your teacher while you gain your sea legs for this new, more fluid way of living. Be gentle and patient with yourself. As with any biological process, it takes the time it takes. There's no use trying to rush it. In the next chapter, we'll look further at this state of enlightenment.

22

The Extraordinary Ordinariness of Enlightenment

Let's assume you have gone through this long process of awakening in all its dimensions. First, congratulations! You have taken a journey that few dare begin, let alone see all the way through.

You have opened your heart to Universal Love and allowed that ecstasy to flow through you and bless all who come into your presence. You feel oneness with all creation and all beings and wish only to fill them with your Love. You give profusely, and the more you give, the more you have to give. You are an inexhaustible source of support for all, truly a gift to life, an offering of the Divine. You fully allow the energy of Creation to flow through your body and animate you and all around you. You pulse with Eros, and your vitality and sensuality enliven all who come into contact with you. You know you are not your body; nevertheless, you occupy it and feel it as never before. You fill it with the vibrant energy of Eros.

You know yourself to be Consciousness/Presence. You know you are infinite and timeless and are that which existed before creation. This deep space of knowing informs your actions, and you display a wisdom that far exceeds your experiences or learned knowledge.

You live in the flow of life and in surrender to what is. Your will is used to navigate that flow, not fight against it. Some traditions call it the *bliss of awakening*.

You have done the hard work to disappear yourself. You have separated yourself from your past and memories. You are not the story of you. You do not dwell in fanciful futures. You see reality as it truly is and no longer dwell in your virtual world. All of you is attentively present to here and now, this present moment. The fullness of you is at hand to address whatever arises.

You understand that being awakened is not a particular state or feeling. It is not a "high." It is the "new normal." In this new normal, you will feel and experience everything you experienced in the unawakened condition, but how you respond will likely be very different.

In the beginning of the book, I quoted Sri Chinmoy: *Do you want to change the world? Then change yourself first.* I paraphrased this to: "First, change your Self to be the world." And so you have. You know that you and existence are one. There is only the Unity. You are not separate from anything. It is all God. At the same time, you live in the paradox that you are also a small creature. That mystery will ever accompany you, for truly, even in the awakened condition, there is no end to the mysteries of the Divine.

Yes, you have come a far, far distance to arrive at these understandings. But even though you have journeyed to the far reaches of the universe, you also know you have gone nowhere.

You are right where you began. You have arrived at the beginning. And having done this journey, you, the prodigal daughter, sense that you have always known what you discovered on the journey. More than a process of exploration, it now feels more like you have simply remembered, as if a fog lifted and a sort of amnesia departed, and you are again standing in front of the home in which you have always lived.

Yes, you may have all the sensibilities listed at the start of this chapter. But you are the same you that you have always been. The essential essence of you is unchanged. You are the same; it is just as if you have awakened from a dream.

Hence the term I prefer: awakening. You have awakened to You. You know the utter ordinariness of the awakened condition. It is nothing extraordinary, not a dizzying intoxication; it feels…well…normal. The amazing adventure I spoke about at the beginning of the book has simply been a homecoming. It is only when you look at the condition in which others live that you can be reminded that you have indeed undergone a profound transformation.

Now What?

When enlightenment is discussed, it is often spoken of as if it is an ultimate destination, the final resting place for a human. But that is far from the case. When one has stabilized in the awakened condition, it marks the beginning of a journey, not an end. Indeed, such awakening could be seen as your "second birth."

Think of the analogy of an astronaut who has left her home planet on a long journey from which there will be no return. So it is with our spiritual explorer. In order to awaken, you have left your past and the personality you knew, relinquished any future you may have dreamed of, let go of the idea that you are your thoughts and emotions or that you are a separate entity. Now there remains only you, naked in this moment.

Imagine that you are this astronaut stepping out of your spaceship onto a brand new planet, a vast space to be explored, where nothing is known. That is you, who will have to learn how to live on this planet as a new being. You will face all the challenges and opportunities that other explorers have faced and, in that regard, nothing has changed. It is only you who are different, and you will learn how to navigate this world from that deeper identity. That world is called Earth.

Utterly normal, completely different. What will you do with that life?

Compassion for Humanity

As an Awakened Being, you have likely persevered through a long journey of challenges and sacrifices to reach this domain. If you now decided to put your legs up and relax into a life of ease, hey, no one could blame you. You've earned it. But most awakened people are not content merely to bask in the rewards. No, they feel a call to help others.

Enlightenment provides a completely different perspective on life from that of an ego-based identity. Radically different. You've probably encountered a mentally ill person on the street. You see them talking to themselves, talking to someone not there and in a time no longer present. Maybe you feel pity or compassion, perhaps a tinge of revulsion, or possibly gratitude that you are not in that situation, or maybe all of these feelings.

When a person who has reached enlightenment listens to ordinary, sane people, hearing what they talk about and feel, listening to the content of their conversations, that awakened person experiences them much like you would experience a deluded, mentally ill person. The enlightened one would, of course, never negatively judge people living in conventional consciousness, but her heart would ache for them. She would see people lost in a fantasy world of their own making, not present to reality. Most of all she would feel the suffering, the unnecessary suffering of millions and millions of people who do not know who they truly are, who have no sense of their own Holiness and greatness. She would feel the pain and heartache resulting from actions taken by these people, each living in his or her own self-serving fantasy world.

When you have awakened, you are touched to your core by the plight of humanity and all creatures. Though there is security and serenity arising from your immovable core, there is no escape from the suffering you feel in those around you. That openness to the needs of others often compels the Awakened One to action in the world. This is what we will address in Part III.

PART III

BECOMING A SAVIOR

Introduction to Part III

Up to this point in the book, we have been focused on individual transformation, your awakening to the Oneness of existence as the Goddess. Now we will turn to world transformation and the role that the Awakened Woman can play in the evolution of life-space on our planet.

The previous chapters provided an overview of the process of spiritual awakening. For any woman or man to reach the awakened state is an enormous and rare accomplishment. Further, to allow that state to season and mature and so take permanent root in the life of the individual is rarer still. For those who have awakened to their Divine nature and who have fully integrated this condition into their life's expression, there is often the question "Now what?"

The answer to that question does not come from the ego but from the dimension of Spirit. It will not be a one-time question, but will be how the person lives from day to day or, as it has been more poetically described: practicing the presence of god. Most awakened people gravitate toward a life more fully in service to the needs of others, some in humble pursuits and some as leaders. The key factor is not the magnitude or type of service, however; it is listening to what Spirit asks of you and faithfully answering the call.

Though your guidance must come from deep within, please permit me in the following chapters to passionately outline a critical unmet need of humanity. I hope my words will stimulate your inner Divine Muse and help you discover how you can best be of service to your fellow humans and our planet.

Our world is awash in problems, significant and seemingly intractable problems. It is my belief that these problems exist primarily because of the excessive influence of the masculine and the suppression of the feminine in most of the world's cultures. Part III examines the root cause of the current slate of global problems and the need for feminine empowerment, in particular, the need for Divinely Awakened Women.

You will note in the following chapters that I am highly critical of male leadership and the damaging consequences of the patriarchal supremacist system that humanity has suffered under for many millennia. Yes, I acknowledge there has been some improvement in the treatment of women over the past century, but my focus is on what is needed still. I also want to acknowledge that some men are conscious of the need for women's empowerment, and such individuals should feel free to except themselves from the broad comments made about men in this next section.

Whether or not you resonate with my observations, I hope you will not dismiss whatever benefits you received from reading the previous chapters of the book. In other words, you can judge each part on its own merits, as this Part III stands on its own and is of a different nature from the rest of the book.

Without further ado, let us move from the individual perspective and shift our focus to the "view from space" on the current human condition.

23

Calling All Women

Women, help! We need you. Our world needs saving. Humanity needs a savior. Actually, we need millions of saviors. It is my conviction that only women can fulfill that essential role, and the women most qualified to redeem humanity will be those who have awakened to their Divine Essence. These Awakened, Enlightened Women may be the saviors of us all, our redeemers.

> HELP WANTED: Everywoman. Home Keepers for Earth. Must keep premises safe for all. Have concern for children's needs and development, ability to manage resources, resolve conflicts, work collaboratively, ask questions, listen, and learn from the experience of others, be empathic, and act with compassion for the benefit of all, including generations to come.
> *Reprinted with permission from* Urgent Message from Mother *by* Jean Shinoda Bolen

It cannot have escaped your attention that our world is awash in problems. Everywhere we turn and at every level—

local, national, global—there are problems aplenty, many of which appear intractable. Here's a brief sampler list, in no particular order:

- Global warming and sea-level rise
- Exploding population growth
- Hunger, poverty, and the "wealth gap"
- Terrorism
- Crime
- Job scarcity and insecurity
- Increasing pandemics
- Species extinction
- Racial, ethnic, and religious strife
- Civil wars
- Rising national debts
- Labor exploitation & slavery
- Air, soil, and water pollution
- Drug dependence
- Addiction to carbon-based fuels
- Traffic congestion
- Fast pace of modern life
- Political corruption, both legal and illegal
- Water scarcity and pollution
- Wars between nations
- Gender discrimination
- Corporate greed and unchecked power
- Collapsing family structure
- Expense of modern medicine
- Inhumane treatment of food animals
- Propaganda power of mass media
- Depleting fisheries
- Soil erosion and increasing salinity
- Dependence of political candidates on ultra-wealthy campaign donors
- Third-world indebtedness to rich nations
- Excluded persons; undesired and exploited minorities
- Dependence of agriculture on chemicals
- Alienation and anomie
- Public expense of supporting senior citizens
- Massive urban mega-slums
- Consumer debt burden
- Genetically altered foods
- Globalization of trade
- Power of large financial institutions
- Emergence of "superbugs"
- Unresponsive, out-of-touch governments
- More "affordable" weapons of mass destruction
- Acidification of the oceans
- Perverse persistence of seemingly easily solvable problems

And the list could go on and on and on. Steps to solve one problem often exacerbate others or create brand-new problems. Even honest government officials are overwhelmed at the sheer number, scale, and difficulty of issues. The quantity and scope of problems seems to be growing, not declining, as humanity "progresses."

Of course, our leaders offer solutions, which typically are hastily and shallowly conceived, with no enduring value, which must pander to entrenched special interests and often leave a new set of problems in their wake.

Instead of dashing around from one problem to another problem in a "whack-a-mole" fashion, wouldn't it be far more efficient and effective if we could dig down and find more fundamental causes from which these myriad problems emerge and deal with those source points? Could it even be possible to find an "alpha point," a place of single origin, from which the world's problems arise? If such a "first cause" exists, could humanity then gain leverage in our common efforts to solve the vast array of problems facing us?

In this chapter, I postulate just such a "first cause" and believe that if this understanding was embraced and disseminated, the quality of life on this planet could make a major leap forward.

For many years, it perplexed me that, though many great thinkers were able to characterize accurately and often brilliantly the myriad problems plaguing humanity today, almost all fell short when it came time to use their insights to offer effective solutions or predict the future. Insight about today did not lead to foresight and wisdom about tomorrow. At best, I saw imagination at work, but not vision. What, I thought, could be the limiting mindset that all these experts had in common? What was the shared reality that blinded their ability to see ahead? What was the nature of the unseen, omnipresent "water" that these "fish" swam in?

Their backgrounds, cultures, education, and experiences were diverse, so what did they have in common? All that I could see was one thing: They were invariably male.

And therein lay the most important clue.

It's a Man's World

All of us live in a world built by men, for men. Not built for men, women, and children, but for men. From Afghanistan to Austria, from Ukraine to the United States, from Rio and Jakarta to Paris and Nairobi, we all live in a world designed, constructed, ruled, and consumed by men—men of every race, faith, and creed. For the past five thousand years and more, women have been mostly barred from participating in this construction project. It has been almost exclusively an all-male club.

It is a world of vicious competition and aggression, an immoral, often-violent world in which greed and the lust for power are the fundamental governing energies, and mistrust and domination are the order of the day. It is a world where nature is plundered and raped for the most vile and banal purposes, a world where billions of humans are economically exploited on a daily basis. All these are simple facts of life. It may be shocking to hear it all stated so bluntly, so inured and resigned have we become to this state of affairs. We have become "normalized" and thus numbed to living.

Even in the so-called "advanced" countries ostensibly governed by the "rule of law," the laws themselves are made by powerful elites and enforced by threat, and the state deems itself justified in exerting whatever level of force is needed to maintain obedience to its laws. Even if the first steps of enforcement are mild, these initial measures are backed up by threats of ultimate violence: injury, incarceration, exile and death.

So alien are these laws from the true wishes and nature of people that if the threat of state violence was removed, the entire structure of laws would collapse. Rather than seeing the entire system as illegitimate and unnatural, however, we place the blame on human nature: Humans require strong-man rule; otherwise, we would create anarchy.

This state of affairs is so natural to us that we have difficulty imagining that it could be any other way. It is a common shared, though unexamined, assumption that this state of affairs is inevitable, that the world can be no other way. We believe that this reflects our human nature, our biological heritage. The world was not always like this, however, though that fact is obscured from public view.

At around five thousand years ago, a revolution in human culture took place, a kind of evolutionary mutation in our psyche. For tens of thousands of years, most of humanity lived a fairly egalitarian, agrarian lifestyle, and for hundreds of thousands of years before that, a foraging style of life. Men did not dominate women the way they do now. In fact, the supreme deity in those earlier days was almost invariably female, and the feminine was honored and respected. Beginning about five thousand years ago; however, a complete revolution in gender relations took place, resulting in the patriarchal domination of women that has been the case since those times.

Intellectuals of various persuasions have offered various theories as to why this transformation took place—from invasions by nomadic warrior horsemen or the invention of the plow, the increased complexity of society, Engel's theories on private property, or the widespread adoption of writing. Whatever the cause(s), historians have traced the migration of this new "idea" over the span of a few thousand bloody years until it came to dominate most of the world. From then on, only men would rule.

The historical recounting of this transformation has been well tilled by a number of academic disciplines and is beyond the scope of this book. An Internet search will lead you to a plethora of sources. One classic book that I recommend on this topic is *The Chalice and the Blade* by Riane Eisler. In the next chapter, we will delve into the deeper currents of the psyche that I believe brought about this dark madness in men.

The Rule of Men through domination is actually a constructed system, a huge system through which our entire world functions. Though comprehensive, it is still only a system, a system created and maintained by humans. Think of it as a giant machine, a machine that requires power to run, resources to consume, and maintenance to keep it working. In this way, it is very different from natural systems. Natural systems are able to self-maintain and self-generate.

The system of male dominance is not an organic, living system. Like all machines built by men, it requires constant intervention, repair, and "management" to keep it working. It does act like a natural system in one respect, though: It will do anything to survive. Like an organism, this system intends to keep on living. The Rule of Men system has only one way to keep living: Keep men dominant.

The Rule of Men system sees the entire world as a giant playing field (or combat arena) in which men can act out their competitive and aggressive impulses. The rule book for this world system is very simple: *To the victor go the spoils.* It is deemed legitimate to have this as the supreme priority. This is the true worldview of dominant men: that the world and everything in it are there to serve their testosterone-driven urges for power, glory and wealth. All other goals, aspirations, and priorities of humanity must be subordinated to this prime directive of the world-dominating system. Every person, creature, and natural resource is hostage to this system and may be drafted into its service, at any time, at the whim of dominant players.

Men want it this way. The dominant, aggressive ones do, anyway. Their naked motivation is most often hidden behind self-serving propaganda, intended to whitewash men's motives so that they appear pure and defensive. It is a world based on Thanatos, not Eros, a system based on reverence of death, not life.

Humanity has lived this way for many generations now, for so long the knowledge that people could live differently has almost vanished from the Earth. But life does not have to be this way. It can be different. It has been different. And this fact is one of the deepest secrets that the Rule of Men system will do anything to hide.

There is a problem and it is simply this: If we do not change the Rule of Men, if we do not replace this world system, the future of humanity is threatened and the biosphere of the Earth itself will be traumatized. There are three options for our future: The future will be feminine, it will be Frankenworld, or it will be violently finished.

The Center of the Universe

A few hundred years ago, most of educated humanity had a heliocentric view of reality, that is, people believed the sun was at the center of the universe. Today, we know that view of physical reality is wrong. We actually live on the fringes of a galaxy comprising many billions of suns, one obscure galaxy in a universe of many billions of galaxies.

Today, humanity holds an equally erroneous worldview, but one that has far more consequences than the error of heliocentrism. This erroneous worldview could be called the "male-centric" view of reality.

In this worldview, the human male is at the center of the universe, the normative foundation of existence, and all of reality orbits around this center. The human male looks out through his eyes as center of his universe, and interprets the world. He looks out through his distortions of vanity, pride, fear, confusion, envy, hunger, sexual urgency, discomfort, craving, and aversion and makes his pronouncements that reality is such-and-such a way. He pronounces with certitude, but he ignores the inner state of the pronouncer. He proclaims that what he sees, interprets, and concludes is reality—the truth of existence.

It is childish to believe so foolishly and so unsupported by evidence. For many thousands of years, however, anyone who disagreed with the consensus male-centric worldview was ostracized, banished, or worse. So the males' self-serving and biased pronouncements of reality are today accepted as true.

I could go on and on about this, but I'm sure you have gotten my drift by now. Simply stated, here is my first point: Men have made an awful mess of the world, and it is getting worse by the day.

The second, more important point is: Women, not men, will have to guide us out of this quagmire. Their leadership will be very different from how men have defined leadership. Women's leadership will be more communal and will seek consensus and inclusion. It is quiet leadership, and the goal is a solution that works for everyone. It will not be Joan of Arc in her masculine armor, leading warring troops on her charging steed. No, it will be grass-roots leadership, life-affirming leadership, leadership by example, leadership from the heart.

And also, I hope, divinely empowered leadership, which I pray I have inspired you to embrace.

24

The Religion of Men
Or: Why Men Can Never Be Environmentalists

Let's begin this chapter with the premise of the previous chapter: The Earth has a problem. It has a problem that is killing it, or more precisely, killing the life on it and driving the current mass extinction event. Many scholars and scientists have devoted much time to the analysis of the differences between the sexes, the history of the rise of male dominance, the current reemergence of the feminine, and prognostications about the future of male-female relations. I would like to discuss only one aspect of this great evolution of humanity, which I believe has not received the emphasis it deserves. Though I am not an anthropologist, historian, economist, archaeologist, or an expert in the other academic disciplines that have plowed this topic, as a spiritual teacher I have access to a perspective that is not normally available to such specialists. There is a spiritual understanding about the male ego that I believe will shed some additional light on the causes of male dominance, on our relationship with the environment, and on the need for feminine spiritual awakening.

On this planet live some 3¾ billion human males, and that number is increasing rapidly. The majority of them are young, quick to aggress, and have idle time to fill. Though their societies span the globe and may be as different as different can be, these men have one thing in common, a value that most have never really thought about, for it dwells in their deep subconscious mind and is not voiced in daily conversation.

What they share is resentment. They harbor a grievance, a sense of inflicted injury, and an urge for retribution. This sense of grievance is fundamental to their maleness and transcends their various societies' values, beliefs, and religions. In fact, it could be said to be the religion beneath the overt religions, a kind of meta-religion shared by most males on the planet. They do not articulate it, for it is too basic to their existence and male identity to be expressed as a distinct thought or statement, but it exists nevertheless as an undercurrent that affects everything they think and do.

The resentment is resentment of life itself. And the (unconscious) rallying cry of that religion is "Death to Life!"

Though this feeling is deep and fundamental, it is not intrinsic to being male. It has not always been this way nor is it an inexorable route predestined by human evolution. No, it is an invention of the male mind, a mutation that happened so long ago and so subtly, that men have forgotten that they invented it, forgotten even that it exists. Here is the (greatly abridged) story of how this came to pass.

Eternity

To look into a loved one's eyes and see eternity is not only poetry or romance, not just an outmoded religious belief — it is truth. Within every human being, there is a center that exists outside of time, a center that is not limited to this life. It has always existed and will always exist. It is not imaginary; it is real, as real as your hand or heart. Mostly, we live with our attention on our ordinary day-to-day existence, and in that hubbub we may not be in communion with our eternal nature. Nevertheless, it is there, waiting quietly for our return. And so it is in the quiet moments that we can best connect with this part of ourselves. For some, it arises in meditative contemplation or when enraptured by nature's beauty and timelessness. Or in love, in moments of deep love and communion with our beloved, our eternal soul nature rises up into our awareness. But only the Awakened Ones can access this realm at will, while most of us are granted only occasional glimpses.

A Little History

You have always lived. You were physically alive before the pyramids were built. You were walking before glaciers covered much of North America; in fact, you were alive before there was even the continent of North America. You are older than the rocks at the bottom of the Grand Canyon. You have witnessed the rising sun a thousand billion times. You have undergone uncountable transformations, and you have never died.

It has taken the entire age of the Universe to create you today — all that time, unimaginable time, to create you. The body you live in came from a star. Before reproducible life stirred in you, the elements that one day would be gathered to become you first had to be created. The only place they could be created was inside a star. When your mother star died, it exploded, sending life's building blocks out into space. Those primordial elements eventually coalesced here, on Earth, and now make up your body. A star had to die so you could be born. So when someone says they "see stars in your eyes," they are right.

All this time…all this change…just to create you.

Creation of Life

For four billion years, a system of life has resided on this planet, a system of unimaginable complexity, sensitivity, and interrelatedness evolving over incomprehensible spans of time. This system of life is so far beyond humanity's skills that all we can do is tinker with it: Breed a new chicken here, do a little surgery there, conduct a DNA transplant in a lab.

The system of life—nature—continues and evolves through the process of rebirthing, that is, the living entities create the next generation of the species from within themselves and birth that progeny before they pass away and die. So it has gone, for eons and eons and eons, life without end, transformations without end.

Early in the history of life, creatures reproduced simply by dividing themselves. Later, they evolved specialized organs to spawn new generations and began not merely to divide, but also to exchange genetic material with other individuals. Finally, nature created a novel subset of creatures, specialists who could not themselves reproduce, but who would merely supply new genetic material to the reproducers. The members of the species who have the anatomical mechanisms for reproduction and birthing are called "females." Virtually all of the work of continuing this system of life is performed by them. The late-arriving secondary specialists, called "males," have no essential role to play in the continuation of life, save for one function: In most species, they provide for mixing of the genes so that the species can continue to adapt and evolve more rapidly.

Of course, in certain forms of life the males can play secondary, supportive roles. They can assist the female in her tasks by providing food, shelter, and protection. But those contributions of the male, while they may be useful, are not absolutely essential to the system.

We call this system of life "nature." So what we have in nature is a self-perpetuating, self-evolving system of life that is designed to produce females so that it can continue to exist and evolve, and, almost as a footnote, create enough males to keep the gene pool stirred up.

This is the system that created each of us. Our bond with nature is only "natural" because, after all, we are She.

Man vs. Nature

The task of birthing and sustaining new life has always been pretty much a full-time job for the females of any species, whether a finch, fish, or fox. On the other hand, for the males of many species, once they filled their stomachs, there was often plenty of leisure. They used this spare time in various ways: to eat more and grow bigger, fight other males with time on their hands, practice aggression, patrol territories, or try to control a group of females. Little of this activity had much significance for the primary purpose of the species to rebirth itself, but at least it gave the males something to occupy their time and consume their excess energy.

This state of affairs did not threaten nature until thinking—in particular, reflective thinking—came into the picture. As humans evolved, they began to think imaginary thoughts—ideas and concepts. Their thoughts were no longer limited to relating to their environment ("Are the figs ripe yet?" or "Are the tigers prowling tonight?") but now included imagining things that never existed ("What is the meaning of life?" or "What is the negative square root of 16?"). This thinking proceeded to the point where the male could see that some of his fellow humans created new life and others (like him) didn't. Then he had to be able to attribute significance to the birthing act. He had to develop enough awareness to understand that this was what life was all about.

Imagine you are a male in a small, primitive, peaceful tribe. In your world, there are two fundamental mysteries: birth and death. The women give birth, create life. The various village chores are shared — cooking, hunting, planting — but in regard to the grand mystery, the great purpose, what can you do? The men have a distinct disadvantage in status when compared with these goddesses of the birth mystery. There may be some prestige in building a dugout canoe, but that is hardly in the same league as creating new life.

Men could attempt to compensate somewhat by artificially elevating the status of their chores vis-à-vis the women's (i.e., canoe building is more important than firewood gathering, hunting is superior to planting). In fact, all over the world we see these attempts to puff up male vanity. But no matter the success of these social compensations, men had to notice that they were, in fact, less significant. That they understood and accepted this fact is evidenced all over the world by historical artifacts of goddess worship.

Throughout our history, men understood they could intervene in the process of life: they could slaughter an animal or bash somebody's head in and end that life. Some men became very good at that and, perhaps in some circles, this was considered high status: Females can create life; males can end it. But life can be ended in many other ways, including by creatures that are much better at it than men, as well as by accident, dis-ease, and aging. So men did not hold a monopoly on human death, as women did with human birth.

What to do, what to do? Well, since men were bigger and physically stronger, they could make themselves the bosses. Even if the women were the primary agents of evolution, at least men could shove them around. Men could rule the goddesses. That had its compensations, but it still didn't set the scale aright in men's eyes.

Once man's intellect developed enough to understand his role in the process of making babies, some men could concentrate on their reproductive role and accumulate enough females to contribute their genes time and time again. This strategy of the harem was not unique to man. The males of many mammal species, from wild horses to lions to baboons practice this strategy. For a very few human males, it had its rewards, but still...

As the dominant men gained more free time, they got better at filling it: better at fighting other men, better at bossing bigger groups, better at creating more complex and demanding chores, better at excluding women from functions that men could perform, and, most importantly, better at inventing explanations for things. This led to their taking charge of the invention of gods, and as the inventors of gods, the creators of gods' rules, and from that, laws, and from that, governance, and from that, cities, states, and nations. Then from those domains, they waged war on other lands and peoples.

Men could rule and construct marvels. Women (forcibly excluded by men from participating in all that) could create life. From the male's viewpoint, this was better, but was it enough? For by this time, man's need for esteem had risen to the need for superiority, for wasn't he now the ruler? His previous sense of inferiority had made him covet control, a desire that at its fundamental core was the desire to control life. If he couldn't create life with his body, at least he could control women's bodies. At least he could invent the world in his image. At least he could destroy the female goddesses and demand obedience to warlike gods created in his image. And as his control over these things grew, he could even fancy himself as a god. A hollow one, yes, for he still could not create life. Since men could not be creators, they would settle for being controllers.

To make this illusion stick required the right combination of sufficient powers of imagination and power over others: the power to rule and compel others to reinforce the ruler's imagination. We have many examples of this: from the emperors of Rome and China to the Pharaohs of Egypt. In fact, it could be said that only in the past century are we (hopefully) leaving the evolutionary era of the age of god-emperors.

To make men seem like gods required that men's activities be most honored, while the process of the creation of life had to be denigrated and diminished. To devalue birthing meant not only that the power of women had to be diminished, but also that nature had to be taken off its pedestal and dishonored. And so it became man vs. nature. Not humanity vs. nature or people vs. nature, but men vs. nature. What came to be honored by men were each of the "triumphs" over nature: both triumphs over nature in the environment and triumphs over our inner nature. In the place formerly held by nature, men honored the "mind" or "intellect."

It was not really the intellect being honored, though, but the ascent of males, of man's ability to plunder nature, to harness nature and rule over it (her) and her most cherished agents (females). Even more fundamentally, men were honoring death in preference to life. They were honoring man's ego and living out their rage against the system of life that insulted their vanity. They were living out man's resentment of his second-class status in fulfilling the essential purpose of life, which is the continuation of the system of life.

Tragically, we are still in this era. The true "religion" at the core of men, the religion that motivates their hearts and minds is anti-life. It is a veneration of death, a theology of death (Thanatos) that has at its core envy and jealousy. Men have gotten quite good at their mission to control and dominate life, leaving a trail of death and destruction in their attempts to invent "constructed and managed" life in its stead. They have taken to their task with great enthusiasm. Enthusiasm powered by the unacknowledged passions of hatred and rage.

"At last we have a proper purpose," they might be saying, as they go about their tasks with great enthusiasm. "We're finally in charge" say the men, in love with man, men valuing man over woman, men acting as gods, constructing their new Dr. Frankenstein world.

It has been said many times that in literature written by men there are three fundamental, recurring themes: man against man, man against nature, man against himself. The operative word here is "against." Really, when you look at the themes men value and admire, aren't they always striving "against" something? What that something may be isn't important, for there will always be something to strive against. The point is that men are striving creatures, and usually striving against, not for.

Even in those themes where a "for" is present ("We will save the world for democracy"), the "for" is usually just the noble excuse to be against something or attain triumph over other males. That something, the thing to strive against, whether the untamed river or the evils of an enemy, is the aspect that truly arouses the passions of men. Isn't destroying or defeating the adversary that is really the true desire, slaying the dragon, not rescuing the princess? No, the princess is just there to make the man feel good about the destroying that he is doing. (But relationship-oriented princesses never seem to understand this about their heroes.)

We have to admit it; men have been very successful in expressing their "anti" nature. But according to most ancient philosophies, that is not their role. Their assigned role is more constructive than just being against. Isn't history full of examples of "successful" revolutions followed by failures to build the "new" society?

Men have gotten stuck in their "against" nature — thoroughly mired in that swamp and having a grand time of it. The problem is that the masculine energy of "striving against" is unlikely to build an enduring environment, community, and world. For that, we need the feminine energy of creation. However, men have excluded women from providing that essential energy.

Are Men Necessary?

In nature, what is the purpose for men? We already know the role given to males by evolution: that of mixing up the gene pool. Is that man's only function? In the bee kingdom, for example, the answer is clear: Only a miniscule number of males are needed to provide a gene pool and, once the drones have fulfilled that mating role, they may be disposed of. But what about human males?

Humans are products of the evolving system of life that has existed for billions of years on our planet. That much is certain. It is also certain that if that system is seriously damaged, we will be destroyed. Therefore, whatever other purposes are inherent or invented by man, his role in preserving nature must be embraced. As even that basic responsibility is not being fulfilled, let us leave the question of whether there are other or higher roles and responsibilities for men until the primary purpose is being honored. And when we do turn to those questions, let answers come from women, for their needs as well as nature's must first be satisfied.

Men, of course, have a core psychological fear that there will be no purpose for them. This fear is so deep-seated that it cannot even be spoken. So they continue to act, but act from animalistic passions, not from a reflective and responsible place, running from the feared truth that they have no purpose, running and remaining transfixed in their fascination with death.

To satisfy themselves that they have a purpose, men keep creating conditions in which their natural abilities are needed. This is most clearly illustrated in men's never-ending creation of conflict: war, politics, business, and competition in games. Men are always causing wars and doing so for their own selfish purposes. Men honor war-makers above all else. Read any history text and what you see is a history of conflicts. This fixation on creating conflict in wars and in its surrogate enterprises (business, politics, and sports) so completely engrosses the attention of men that few will ever have to face the most-dreaded thought: "Are we even necessary?"

The Religion of Men: Death to Life!

To protect themselves from thoughts that they might be inferior to women in the natural order of things — or even unnecessary — men invented religious and philosophical systems to justify their revolution and secure their status. The Judeo-Christian-Islamic religions, for example, are all a reflection of this purpose. All raise man's ego to a sacred level and justify his domination of women and nature.

This history that we have been describing must be understood before there will be any hope of remedying the major problems facing the world today. The great majority of the world's current problems were created by a dangerous mutation, a usurper system that has attempted to overthrow the four-billion-year-old system we call nature. The usurper system, an invention of the male ego that has as its core purpose the ascent of man's ego over nature's organic life-creation system, is far from having run its course.

Scholars can debate whether this development was inevitable or had net positive outcomes. Just as a boy must separate from his mother in order to establish his separate identity, some would say that the collective male identity had to separate from Mother Nature and stand separate from her. Similarly, this point of view holds that humanity was "embedded" in nature and that it was essential and inevitable for humanity to be able to rise above her in order to allow our intelligence and vision to develop free from the more unified state we lived in while so embedded. My focus is not on such historical speculation. Mine is more focused on the future. Male dominance and estrangement from nature, whether necessary in the past or not, is now a dangerous condition that cannot be allowed to persist.

It is now at its most dangerous point. One might think the past 50 years or so were the most dangerous, when humanity stood at the brink of nuclear annihilation. But that drama merely signaled the beginning of the end of an era that was, in reality, only a prelude to the true goal of the religion of men. In that first era men focused on fighting with other men for dominance. As noted earlier, this has always been a way for males to occupy their time and attention, but defeating other men and collecting the spoils of conquest, as satisfying as it may be, is not the ultimate goal of the religion of death.

Many men will no doubt continue that pastime for some centuries to come. The best and brightest understand, however, that the war game, like tic-tac-toe, cannot ultimately be won. The more insightful ones see the true opportunity and mission. With their focus reframed, men can now turn their attention to their ultimate objective: *the control of life itself in all its aspects.*

It is the values of this "religion" that are the root source of the problems the world is facing today, and it is those same values that underlie men's attempts to solve those problems. Thus it is assured that the solutions will only create greater problems down the line. It is also assured that these solutions will diminish life and nature.

Men's Political Control of Life

With this understanding about men, it becomes easier to understand men's unacknowledged (and perhaps unconscious) motivations underlying many of today's social conflicts. For example, let's consider men's resistance to the women's liberation movement and other efforts to bring about equality for women. The problem is not merely about sharing household chores or equal access to jobs but about the threat the movement poses to the entire existence of the religion of death. Man's religion, dominant as it is, is built on a psychological house of cards. In the deep psyche of each man is the awareness of his inferior status. Man's vanity is further bruised by the memories he retains of his utter dependence on his mother in his early years and his subsequent rejection of her. (Of course, these are painful thoughts only because man strives to maintain the illusion of his superiority. If he did not need to do so, he could celebrate, for example, how he has been cared for and nurtured by the feminine.)

Understanding this meta-religion helps us to illuminate men's extreme passion for a number of issues that clearly do not warrant such vehemence. Let's begin with the anti-abortionists. This political advocacy group has demonstrated repeatedly that they have little regard for the welfare of living children, while wailing their concern that "babies" are being killed. Their "feel good" justification cannot disguise the true motivation that arouses their indignation and wrath, which is women having control over their own bodies and birth. This issue, in turn, is at the core of the war between man and nature/woman: *Who controls the creation of life?* For men, of the roughly 20 years of dedicated effort that it takes to conceive and nurture a new generation of humans, the moment of sperm implantation (his signature role) is the almighty event that must be worshipped and protected.

We can also better understand the extremity of the illogical passions against evolution as humanity's creation story, rather than the biblical story of Genesis. The god of Genesis created men first and made them the masters of women, end of story; whereas, in nature and evolution, late-arriving men have only a pitifully small importance. It is not Christian devotion that feeds men's fervor against Darwin and evolution, but the panic of a cornered ego facing an unacceptable truth.

Men's hatred of male homosexuals can also be seen in this light. Almost all men are very insecure in their male identity, so to have some men actively favor more feminine expressions or even reject being men will enrage to frenzy men whose identity is threatened by such "breaking of the ranks." Their wrath is of the kind reserved for traitors and turncoats.

The failure of the environmental movement can likewise be understood. Men can never be environmentalists. They can never be truly "for" nature because they are at war with her. This war constitutes a foundation for their identity. Of course, there are some men who feel they do support the environment. Even in those cases, however, their masculine proclivities often render their actions ineffective or counterproductive. Men's natural protective instincts can sometimes be stimulated to action for the environment, but this sets them into David versus Goliath conflicts where the stronger party will tend to win. Here is yet another example that illustrates it is the fight that matters to these crusaders. The "environment" is merely the stand-in for the fair maiden.

For women, the relationship with nature is much more intimate. Women feel and sense nature. They can love nature as a beloved, or even feel nature as an extension of themselves. Rare indeed is the man who can act from so intimate a relationship with nature. Men's mission, their "religious duty," is to destroy that organism *in its entirety* and replace it with one manufactured by their egos—the Frankenstein world: Frankenworld.

Men clearly understand at a deep level of knowing, even if they do not allow the thought to enter their conscious minds, that there can be only one of two outcomes: either revert back to the way things were (i.e., be the less-important sex) or build an entirely new world designed by men's egos, a world in which man's wounded pride rules over and directs life, a world in which men continue to be more important than women and can dominate them.

Creating Tomorrow

If men remain in charge, we can't expect our future to look any different. While the past several hundred years have seen unprecedented technological change, the inner human has changed little, if at all. The natural instincts of the masculine have two inevitable results: war and the creation of deserts. Warfare has been constant and of a different nature since men broke their partnership with women. That violent tendency, when coupled with the technologies of destruction, will lead us to our ruin. As long as men remain the unchallenged leaders of our societies, we will continue to see unending armed conflicts. Recent centuries have seen record-setting numbers of casualties from warfare. Scholars can debate whether the number and impact of such conflicts is increasing or decreasing, but whatever the trends, the consequences of those conflicts could potentially be more catastrophic and lethal. If men are settling their differences with stone axes and arrows, that is one thing, but war is no longer contested with such primitive instruments. Even the widespread availability of personal transport coupled with two simple, inexpensive weapons—assault rifles and rocket-propelled-grenades—has dramatically increased the lethality of even impoverished combatants. With modern militaries, we see civilization-ending power. Sooner or later, the use of weapons of mass destruction will be irresistible to one faction or another, and their civilizations will be devastated.

In addition to warfare, the other danger that humanity faces from leadership by men is the reckless use of technology. As noted earlier, men simply cannot let nature be. They are too uncomfortable with nature and are hell-bent on building a world that they can comprehend and control. Men have an instinct for plunder, taking whatever is in their grasp. You can also count on them to act from myopic self-interest, and let the broader and long-term consequences be damned. Men cannot curb their appetites. They must have more, more, more. This instinct also governs men's relationship with nature: Take whatever you can from her. When nature provides men with a resource, you can count on them depleting it. Inevitably, we achieve the ability to take more than nature can sustainably provide, and so a part of her dies. She can provide no longer. What once was abundant with life becomes a desert denuded of life.

Intelligent men now understand that their appetites will always be more powerful than nature can sustain. So men are busily building a replacement for nature. They are piece-by-piece manufacturing a life-system to replace her. Like Dr. Frankenstein, they are fabricating their version of life: Frankenworld. If we look around, we can see it being constructed: Life-creation is moving into the laboratory and away from natural breeding; personal communication is now mediated through media forms rather than conducted personally; baby formula must replace the breast; plants and animals must be designed in laboratories and grown in factories, not fields and oceans; the hospital must replace the bedroom for birthing and dying; artificial organs must replace natural ones worn out by unhealthy eating of unnatural foods; constructed life forms must replace inferior natural organisms; and soon, even humans will be designed from specifications, and then one day (oops!) involuntarily replaced by a new species designed by men. You can continue this list in your head. It is endless.

This machine will get bigger and bigger, with bits of it breaking down from time to time, as machines will. But it will keep growing, and we will become more and more dependent on it. One day it will encompass everything…and then it will irrevocably break. It will not be repairable, and Frankenworld will catastrophically collapse in on itself. Many dystopian movies are variations on this theme. Art precedes reality.

In order for their egos to be satiated, men have to *improve* on nature. Since nature has not honored men to their satisfaction, nature ipso facto must be flawed, and men must set her "right."

Therefore, men will build a world of their design in which they are essential and in which they can rule. But since men cannot create or rule nature, she must be destroyed and be replaced by a world of man's own construction in which he *can* rule.

These are not unalterable trajectories that humanity must take, but are trends solely created by the masculine mind, a mind cut off from the feminine and from nature, a mind intoxicated by hubris and bereft of humility. Left to men, the future will be a Frankenstein nightmare, and the construction of that future is well under way.

Thus we see two outcomes if men remain in charge: a future that is consumed by violence or a future that is Frankenworld. Let us next turn to an alternate future, one that is feminine.

25

Birthing the New World

In the last chapter, we saw that the future will be feminine, Frankenworld, or finished, depending on how humanity chooses to deal with our state of crisis. Destruction by conflict or through Frankenworld are the two futures that the masculine can offer us. If humanity is to avoid these catastrophes it will require a fundamental pivot away from the masculine and toward the feminine. The world has been unbalanced toward extreme masculinity for far too long. It is time to set the balance aright. The future must be more feminine. Men may have built the civilizations in which we live, but throughout history, it is the women who create communities and families.

Women create and nurture life. That is certainly true at the individual level; we form, live, grow, and gain awareness under a mother's protection and care. Women also tend and nurture nature. They are the growers and gardeners, the tenders of life.

As the consciousness of humans evolves, many spiritual teachers tell us that our collective consciousness affects the life system of the world. The planetary life form is evolving, and a new level of consciousness wants to come into Earth's life system, these teachers tell us. This prediction is not merely some new-age fantasy; it is coming from many diverse wisdom sources. Shamanic leaders from around the world are saying this, as are many awakened adepts and even a number of scientists.

It is women who have the natural attunement to this potentiality, for they are inextricably enmeshed in the potential of new life, whether an individual infant, a garden, or the planetary life form. For convenience, let's call that life form Gaia (or Gaea), the name given by the Greeks to the mother goddess of the Earth.

There is a music of creation in the universe and a music of life sung by Gaia. Awakened adepts can feel it and harmonize their actions with it. Women's bodies also feel this music. Most women's minds are not conscious of this; they feel it only instinctively. Once they open their consciousness through spiritual practice, however, they quickly sense this music and act (dance) in harmony with it. If humanity is to successfully address the multitude of problems we face, our actions will have to be in accord with the natural music of life.

Most men, by contrast, are oblivious to this potentiality. They are still busily playing out their adolescent power fantasies, using the planet as their game space. This has to stop, and soon. Even for men who are not involved in such destructive activities and who are committed to the advancement of humanity, their life-energy systems are not as naturally attuned to Gaia. They cannot hear or understand her. Even if their intentions are good, they will be groping blindly in the dark.

When a problem persists and men attempt to solve it, their natural tendencies will lead them to more dysfunctional, fabricated systems. They will always be looking for a better technology, structure, mental concept, ideology or some other "ism" to "fix" things. They then impose their fabricated constructions onto the unchanged human.

Men cannot hear the music of Gaia, so they need to learn to become more humble and offer their skills to implement solutions provided by women, who can hear Gaia's song. This would be a big shift for men. Men want to lead and solve problems their way. Man's whole motivational system is oriented to the fight to get to the top so he can rule. This energy is played out in the macrocosm and microcosm, from the home to the workplace to the nation state. In a man's view, the all-important issue is who gets to be the boss.

The feminine does not want to lead in this way; she does not want to be the "boss lady." She wants everyone to be satisfied; she wants everyone to win. Life for her is not a competition. She instinctively feels the needs of the people and planet, and she wants to meet those needs. She requires in men partners who will listen and honor her instinctive knowing. If men then act consciously and humanely in accordance with her knowing, she is satisfied. They can take the credit for all she cares; it is the result that is important to her.

Many thousands of years ago this essential partnership was lost when men wanted to be the sole actors in life. Since that mutation spread, life has been less alive and vibrant. Until the last few centuries, however, it was not a threat to humanity at large or to Gaia. Humans had little more power than beasts, so their actions, no matter how ill-advised or locally tragic, did not have the scale of impact that could jeopardize larger systems of life. Now, though, technology has provided humans with immense power, and the cumulative impact of our actions is having devastating and far-reaching consequences.

The old patriarchal system is coming to its inevitable end. That is certain, as it contains within it the seeds of its own destruction. The question is whether humanity can safely transition to a new system or whether the decline will play out until we reach the point of catastrophic collapse.

Because of the dangers to humanity that stem from the system of male dominance and the growing understanding of the natural biological superiority of women, there are writers who believe that men will soon be overshadowed by women and that men will be relegated to the sidelines or found to be unnecessary in the future. Of course, this is exactly what men fear. (There are a number of books along this theme, beginning with the classic written over a half century ago, *The Natural Superiority of Women,* by Ashley Montagu, as well as more recent contributions from anthropologists, psychologists, and other academics, as well as feminists.)

I take a somewhat different view and see a potential for the growth of a more natural and powerful woman-man partnership. Yes, the system of male dominance must be dismantled and women's voice must be heard in world, community and family affairs, but that will address only part of the problem. The other force that needs to be addressed if the future is to be any different from the present is intrinsic to the nature of the ego.

The rule of the masculine is more precisely described as the rule of the masculine ego. If we simply replace the masculine ego with the feminine ego, that will no doubt offer some improvement. The fundamental anti-life instincts of men will be moderated to some degree. An ego is still an ego, however, and all egos live in a self-absorbed, simmering stew of desire, fear and delusion. Given this inherent limitation, having female egos guide humanity will not be a cure-all.

Saviors and Redeemers

What humanity needs in order to rightly chart its future are Awakened Women, women who have done the necessary inner work to transcend their limited egoic identity. In other words, our saviors will be the living Goddesses. It is in these enlightened women that the energy of creation and the music of life is fully experienced and made conscious. In them, instinct is fully expressed as wisdom. If there are "experts" that humanity needs in order to survive and prosper, it is these illuminated women. Only they can be the responsible stewards of humanity.

Today, there are many women in positions of leadership and power. In most cases, though, it is not feminine leadership; it is simply women playing the men's masculine power game. This is not what I mean by feminine leadership. Rather than me explaining that distinction to you, let Awakened Women demonstrate how feminine leadership is unfolding. It is my hope that all women reading this will feel the call, rising from their depths, to awaken themselves as the Goddess and become the saviors of humanity and Gaia. Any Awakened Woman can be such a savior. She does not need to hold a powerful position, as the male model of power would dictate. Most of the true transformative work will be done in humble circumstances—mothers being conscious parents and responsible neighbors—and by Awakened Women transmitting their illumination and love to those around them.

We can't expect that men, particularly men in power, will welcome the return of the feminine in world and community affairs. When anyone has become accustomed to entitlement and privilege, including gender entitlement, they are loathe to relinquish it, feeling that such an advantage is their rightful possession. But men have an even deeper and more profound reason to nding their domination of women in favor of a more balanced partnership. As noted, a man's identity is a shaky, fragile thing. Every woman knows how easily men can interpret even a small criticism or difference of opinion as a threat to their ego structure. For many men, their belief that they are "superior" to and entitled to dominate women constitutes a core foundation of their sense of identity. They see this condition as "natural" rather than a thinly-veiled justification for their entitlement. The refusal of a woman to accept that domination can provoke an existential crisis in these insecure men.

Therefore, one of the great skills Awakened Women will need to possess is the ability to melt that resistance. How they will go about that, I cannot say, for I am a man. But I trust that the instinctive knowing is there, deep in her depths. What aware, responsible men can do, awake or not, is support such women, protect them, and assist them in implementing the needed changes. I hope there will be sufficient numbers of such men.

Truly, Awakened Women pose no threat to men, only to men's exclusive rule. Awakened Women want to work in partnership with men; they want men to be valued and honored. They want to serve the greater good, and what they need from men is to also be honored and trusted and respected.

The dismantlement of the patriarchy does not mean that men will have to become feminized or subservient. Most women have always appreciated and been naturally attracted to "manly" men. But Awakened Women need those men to now be more conscious and value their contributions. She needs them to be willing to forego the unwarranted entitlement that the patriarchal system gives to men. She needs them to express more humility and wisdom in their actions. She needs them to understand that their role is to protect and support the feminine, while deferring to her innate understanding of what life needs from us. She needs true partners.

> **Seeker Story**
> During an exercise, our group of women brainstormed qualities we desired in the various men in our lives, listing different qualities under three categories:
> 1. Lover/playmate (handsome, hard body, amazing lover, rough, tender, unlimited time)
> 2. Partner/husband/father (provider, generous, stable, respectful, loyal)
> 3. Partner in spiritual awakening (wise, devotional, self-actualized, encouraging, supportive)
>
> Yet, eventually, all of these various qualities found their way into the life partner category. It was so illuminating to see the way that we as women collapse the separate roles into one resource—our significant other. And it was so obvious to all of us that there is no super-human on the planet who could offer each and every quality that we come to expect from our partners. Seeing how much we ask from our partners, we must also ask ourselves how much we are willing to bring similar qualities into the relationship in service to our partners. It was exhausting to even imagine. The experience was not only humbling but also generated much compassion for the men in our lives and the heroic contributions they are already making daily to all of us.

You Are the Future

Humanity and Gaia need the awakened feminine. It is only the feminine, in particular the feminine awakened to her Divinity, to her Goddess nature, who can restore the balance to our unbalanced world.

The world needs your heart of unconditional Love. The world needs your feminine life force, your vital, unconstrained

Eros. It needs the wisdom of your awakened consciousness. We all need the nurturance of the living Goddess. We need her power, her vision, her wisdom, her peace.

Men have been building their power for many millennia. Now, rather than attempting to constrict the power of men, women need to claim their full power and rise to meet the aware and responsible male at a new level of partnership. In this partnership, it is the women who must be listened to and revered. The feminine knows life, and the masculine must defer to this knowing. Our redemption lies with her, not him. And not only our redemption, but the doorway into a beautiful future for humanity.

Union with Nature

As we noted above, women are more naturally attuned to nature than are men. Nature, Gaia, badly needs to have humanity's consciousness working with her, not against her. I believe that when individuals spiritually awaken to unity consciousness, their consciousness merges with nature and informs her, and in turn is informed by her. In this merging/marriage, they become one consciousness and through that consciousness become a single organism. When the body awakens as Eros, it also enters union with Nature and experiences oneness with her. Humanity and Nature are no longer separate, but have attained union through marriage. This is the era that is now possible—a conscious species (us) in symbiotic communion with Gaia. A union through which she can sense us (and herself) as never before, and we can intimately sense her.

With this union in place, there will finally be a consciousness powerful enough to end the era of exploitation. The era of selfish, short-term gain trumping long-term sustainability will end.

The era of "me, me, me" will be replaced with responsibility for the collective well-being of all humans and the planetary life-system, Gaia, of which we are a part.

For me, this renaissance is no utopian dream. It is something actually experienced in the awakened condition, a state of relatedness that is known and that informs the actions of the awakened person. History has brought us to this point. We can seize the moment and take ourselves to a new dimension of human experience, and by so transforming ourselves, provide the consciousness that Nature needs in order to further evolve.

Imagine an entire planet living as one intelligent organism, regulating herself much as our body regulates all its parts. You and I can provide essential, missing elements to the brain and nervous system of Gaia. To offer this gift to life requires no special skills and talents, but only that we transcend our separate, confined individual identity and awaken to our Divinity, and from that boundary-less consciousness merge with Gaia. Imagine a planet who not only senses but who is conscious. A true Eden.

In so doing, we will end our self-imposed exile from Gaia. We can once again live in and as her; we can again romp and revel as the creatures we are; we can become the collective consciousness that is grand enough to evolve a world. That future awaits. We have only to reach for it and keep reaching until we are Home in our Holy Garden once again.

The Power of Love

If Awakened Woman is to assume this sacred responsibility, she will first have to undergo a great sacrifice that will require all the courage and love she can muster. The sacrifice is this: to forgive men. Over thousands of years of patriarchy and misogyny, men have run roughshod over women, often brutally, even to the nt of treating them as little more than slaves or livestock.

omankind's list of legitimate grievances could be endless, and it is understandable that many women could have a great fear and loathing of men. If women are to take their place as the healers of humanity and Gaia, however, their fear, mistrust, hatred, and rage cannot have a place in the DNA of the new world. That infection cannot be passed on to the generations to come. The Love that abides in Awakened Women must be called on for a great act of forgiveness of men so that the new world can be born free from the past grievances of women. Healing is what is needed, not vengeance.

This sacrifice will be all the more challenging because women will be forgiving not only past insults but current and future ones as well, because most men are still living in an untransformed state. This will not be a one-time forgiveness, but a continuing flow of forgiveness after forgiveness after forgiveness, while humanity undergoes the transition from masculine to feminine stewardship. Just as a mother cannot expect gratitude from her three-year-old for what she provides that infant, she cannot expect men to ask for this forgiveness, or understand or appreciate it, or even be aware of it.

Only the greatest Divine Love could bear this sacrifice, but such devoted love abides deep in the heart of every woman. The gift of each woman is to awaken that Love and courageously dare to offer it. She will not be able to dominate men into this new future, but she can love them and entice them into it. That love and allure will be what men need in order to overcome their own fear of the change.

They will not be the first beneficiaries of this forgiveness. You will. In forgiving thusly, the freedom of Love will be yours; and with it, the merging of your heart with the Love that illuminates the Universe.

Seeker Story

Richard has often shared with us that women have plenty to be angry about. He has also stressed the importance of forgiveness. His invitation to us has been to forgive men for all their past transgressions, historically through eons of generations as well as in our current lives. The magnitude of that invitation became clear to me on a very personal level as I contemplated the need to forgive my ex's behavior. I finally understood the enormity of my resentment and the commitment it will take to forgive my ex-husband's continuing offenses over and over, again and again. It's an awesome challenge and ongoing practice, and one not for the faint of heart! It makes me weep to wonder if I am courageous enough to be vulnerable and openhearted in the face of wrongdoing. In that challenge, however, I am inspired by the opportunity for my own enlightenment, as well as the potential for humanity to create a very different future.

That future already lives in my feminine. She moves through the world in a pleasurable banquet of the senses. We women are open, relaxed, playful and oriented toward connection and win-win opportunities. Our pace is slower, more supportive and collaborative, and it would be a great service to share this unique perspective with our men. Their masculine might find a much greater appreciation for the messiness, juiciness, joyfulness and imperfection of life. It's a whole new way for men to experience the world, leaning away from their power fixation, and serious, tense ways of being.

We opened *Woman, Goddess & Savior* with these words from the Dalai Lama: *The world will be saved by the Western woman.* This sentiment is being expressed in many forms by visionaries everywhere. A new era, a new stage of evolution, is available to humanity, and only the feminine can guide us there. Everything depends on this. When enough women have ascended to their full Goddess nature, they will call out to be met by awakened God-men. And when the Divine She and Divine He embrace that call, humanity may at last realize the dream of the sacred marriage of the Divine feminine and masculine, *Hieros Gamos*. This Union will awaken a new chapter for our species and Universe, and only the Great Knower can foresee what such a future will bring.

In this new era, neither men nor women will dominate. It will be a time of unprecedented partnership between the genders. Both parties' strengths and assets will be needed. Collaboration will be essential. Enlightened women can build such partnerships.

The world's need for Awakened Women has never been greater. Without them, humanity's challenges may be insurmountable. With them, humanity, the Earth and even the Universe may enter a new chapter. I hope multitudes of women will feel this potential in their hearts and respond. We need a new generation of Goddesses, of Saviors, to birth the new evolution of humanity and a new era for Gaia. I hope your heart will feel that call. I hope you will awaken the sleeping Goddess who lies within, and redeem us all. Gaia and all her children need you; humanity needs you, men need you, women need you, the future needs you.

Please Awaken!

END

Acknowledgments

Something old, something new, something borrowed, something blue. Schools of spiritual awakening have been around for many thousands of years, and some of them have developed comprehensive maps of the awakening process. Like any teacher in this field, I rely heavily on the inspired work product of the many generations of compassionate geniuses who have preceded me. True discovery is rare and usually very incremental in such an ancient art. I hope I have added a small bit of uniqueness with the path that I teach, but that is meager indeed in comparison to the foundation of knowledge on which I stand. Perhaps what we modern-day spiritual teachers can best provide are newer, more relevant ways of communicating this subject to contemporary Western cultures and individuals.

Like any student, I benefitted from the knowledge, wisdom and love of my selfless teachers. In this material I believe they will see the positive contributions they have made to the construction of my own dharma. For such individuals, all the satisfaction they seek is that others may become enlightened. I would, though, like to express my gratitude to my teachers Saniel Bonder and Linda Groves-Bonder who so lovingly held me during the tender infancy of my second birth awakening.

As regards to the polishing and publishing of the book, a number of friends who volunteered their time should be acknowledged. Several read early drafts and offered valuable input regarding readability. They included Lynne, Linda, and Jeanne. Sharon read and also did an early comprehensive proof of the entire work, and Kathleen spent many hours fact-checking.

Another person who deserves my thanks is my long-term friend Malissa, who encouraged me to begin teaching in the first place, and then called on her large network of friends to populate my first working group of students. Everything that has followed, including this book, came from that first spark.

My manuscript editor Stephanie Marohn and my book midwife Ruth Schwartz (aka the Wonderlady) used their professional skills to turn my rough material into the book you have in your hands.

My beloved students also deserve a special acknowledgement. The personal stories that they generously provided, many of them very private and intimate, added a richness and human dimension to the story of awakening.

About the Author

Richard Axial, a business school graduate of one of the world's most renowned universities, enjoyed a successful top-level management career in both commercial enterprises and non-profit organizations, but during this time he always understood that a job is not a purpose. So, more than two decades ago he left that lucrative career in order to follow the call of the Life Divine.

During his subsequent spiritual journey he studied under both male and female teachers. In parallel with his spiritual development, he experienced a growing awareness of the need for women's empowerment in global and community affairs, and the need for greater presence of the Divine Feminine, the Goddess, in the human heart.

As a consequence of these two passions he developed a fresh new path of spiritual awakening specifically designed for modern women, one intended to meet their needs as career women, mothers and householders. The methods and practices of his school stand in significant contrast to the methods typically employed by more traditional spiritual teachers.

As a parallel expression of his commitment to the Divine, from 2005-2015 Richard also served on the governing board of a scientific institute at the forefront of consciousness research, and the knowledge gleaned there has contributed to his unique approach to spiritual awakening.